MAX notes

Homer's

The
Odyssey

Text by
Andrew J. Parks
(B.A., Rutgers University)
Department of English
Drew University
Madison

Illustr
Jame

D1042455

Research & Education Association

MAXnotes™ for
THE *ODYSSEY*

Printed in the United States of America

Library of Congress Catalog Card Number 94-65953

International Standard Book Number 0-87891-943-0

MAXnotes™ is a trademark of
Research & Education Association, Piscataway, New Jersey 08854

What **MAXnotes**™ *Will Do for You*

This book is intended to help you absorb the essential contents and features of Homer's The *Odyssey* and to help you gain a thorough understanding of the work. The book has been designed to do this more quickly and effectively than any other study guide.

For best results, this **MAXnotes** book should be used as a companion to the actual work, not instead of it. The interaction between the two will greatly benefit you.

To help you in your studies, this book presents the most up-to-date interpretations of every section of the actual work, followed by questions and fully explained answers that will enable you to analyze the material critically. The questions also will help you to test your understanding of the work and will prepare you for discussions and exams.

Meaningful illustrations are included to further enhance your understanding and enjoyment of the literary work. The illustrations are designed to place you into the mood and spirit of the work's settings.

The **MAXnotes** also include summaries, character lists, explanations of plot, and chapter-by-chapter analyses. A biography of the author and discussion of the work's historical context will help you put this literary piece into the proper perspective of what is taking place.

The use of this study guide will save you the hours of preparation time that would ordinarily be required to arrive at a complete grasp of this work of literature. You will be well-prepared for classroom discussions, homework, and exams. The guidelines that are included for writing papers and reports on various topics will prepare you for any added work which may be assigned.

The **MAXnotes** will take your grades "to the max."

Dr. Max Fogiel
Program Director

Contents

> **Each book includes List of Characters, Summary, Analysis, Study Questions and Answers, and Suggested Essay Topics.**

Introduction

The Homeric Tradition

The authorship of the *Iliad* and the *Odyssey* has been disputed heavily for decades. Previous tradition held that Homer, the ancient, blind poet who sang of a heroic age that was long past even in his own day, composed these magnificent poems. The epics were then handed down through the generations until they acquired an immortal fame that no other work could ever hope to equal, no less exceed.

Today, these traditions have been blanketed by more than a century of scholarship disputing not only Homer's claim to complete authority over the poems, but even the poet's historical existence. To best understand the arguments on both sides (for indeed the consensus has not swayed unanimously into the realm of total doubt), we must first understand the basis for the Homeric tradition itself.

That the details of Homer's supposed existence vary widely is not surprising, considering the tradition is two and half millennia old. Still, the common theory dictates that Homer lived on the western coast of Asia Minor (in modern-day Turkey) in the city of Smyrna circa the eighth or ninth century B.C. The tradition of the Trojan War, with many of its related stories and episodes, was already several centuries old in Homer's day; his characters and the action that surrounded them would have been known to his contemporaries. Indeed, both poems assume their audience possesses a knowledge of at least the general storyline of Troy.

The irony of Homer's place as the founder of Western literature is that, in all probability, the master bard was himself illiterate. He was a singer of tales in the oral tradition, most likely entertaining at feasts and court occasions to earn his keep. This does not mean that Homer composed a work and then memorized it by rote, for such a thing assumes that he wrote something down that could be memorized verbatim. The oral tradition was much more subtle and complex than that, as can be observed from Yugoslavian poets who still practice their art in our own century.

An apprenticed bard was taught to employ many tools to master the oral poetic medium. There were routine formulas that he manipulated to form the core of his narrative, and he shaped around these formulas a body of story material that he also inherited. He was taught to compose his story in meter, to the accompaniment of a musical instrument such as the lyre; he never composed his stories without the aid of music. When called upon to perform, the bard would often be asked to recite a particular story or episode that was popularly known, but he would in turn compose his own version of the tale extempore.

What this means is that the oral poet never told the same story twice. Every performance was an original one, as formulaic expressions were meshed with wholly original poetry within the structure of a particular story. As time wore on, a bard continually reciting a particular story would begin to tighten up his structure as he became aware of ingredients which were more effective than others, but the story could never be identical from one performance to the next.

What Homer composed, then, was a series of short episodes that could each be recited in a single evening. The entire mass of tradition that Homer accumulated became the core for the two epic poems as we now have them. Disciples of Homer carried on his tradition, adopting the formulaic arrangements that their master had originated and retelling the stories with essentially Homeric elements. It is supposed that a school of Homerites lived on the island of Chios, and from there they brought the Homeric tradition to the Greek mainland. Then, sometime before or during the sixth century B.C., Homer's works reached their final form and were inscribed in writing.

Even within the Homeric tradition itself, we must accept the fact that what we are reading are not the *exact* words of Homer at all. Indeed, even if Homer himself had been capable of writing down his work, we would have only a single performance of Homer; the many variations of his work which took place over the course of his life would be lost to us. As it stands, Homer's legacy consists solely of a tradition which underwent several centuries of revision by later poets. Yet, so integral were Homer's personality and skill to that tradition that his fame as the poems' founder never waned among his descendants.

The written versions of the *Iliad* and *Odyssey* were widely disseminated and known in classical Greece and surrounding regions such as Egypt. The organization of each of the poems into twenty-four separate Books is the invention of later editors and certainly not the work of Homer or his descendants in the oral tradition. For the most part, the tradition of epic poetry in the West stems from these written versions of the Homeric poems. Classical epic poems in Greek and Latin were directly modeled on Homer, although the Augustan Virgil altered the genre in order to suit the needs of his time when he composed the *Aeneid*. Dante knew Homer through Virgil, and both he and (two centuries later) Torquato Tasso Christianized Homeric elements when they composed their respective epics, the *Commedia* and *Gerusalemme Liberata*. Milton's English epic, *Paradise Lost*, is also heavily laced with Christianized elements from Homer.

But consider now those earlier Greek epics, known familiarly as the Epic Cycle and including such poems as the *Thebais*, the *Nostoi*, the *Little Iliad*, the *Destruction of Troy*, and the *Cypria*. There are scattered passages in post-Aristotelian writings that ascribe to Homer the authorship of these works, though it is unlikely that Homer did indeed write them. Many scholars fear that, just as these works have been ascribed erroneously to Homer, so too might one or both of his epics be the work of other poets.

Many scholars, although believing Homer wrote the *Iliad*, propose that either a disciple of his or another poet familiar with his style wrote the *Odyssey*. One reason for this assertion is that the overall structure and style of the poems differs significantly, and the possibility of false authorship attributed to other classical poems strengthens the argument. Other scholars counterargue that any number of poets whose extant works are undoubtedly their own have created works of differing structures. Others have cited the symmetry and similarity of scope existing between the two works, which they assert outweighs any so-called differences in style and structure.

The more radical arguments come from those who believe that, due to the very nature of oral-formulaic poetry, the odds of a real person named Homer ever having existed are minimal. They assert that one or more schools of poets created a vast body of oral literature over the course of many years. These traditions were later compiled and organized by unifying hands. Then, after the *Iliad*, the *Odyssey*, and the various poems of the Epic Cycle had been written and disseminated, the Greeks attributed all of this work to a fictional poet named Homer, the blind poet of Smyrna.

The truth of the matter, of course, is beyond physical proof. Students of Homer should make themselves aware of these various theories, but it is with the poetry itself and not in the historicity of their supposed creator that we should most concern ourselves.

Historical Background: The Trojan War

No student of Homer's poetry can ignore the central event of both the *Iliad* and the *Odyssey*: namely, the Trojan War. Odysseus' journeys take place after his participation in the Greek campaign at Troy. The household troubles which he faces on his return result from his long absence during both the war and the wanderings which follow it. The enormous body of literature devoted to this singular event is a testament to the significance it held in the eyes of both Homer's contemporaries and the generations that followed.

In his poetry, Homer depicts an era which is professedly not of his own time, but of a heroic age long past. The archaeological discovery of Troy by Heinrich Schliemann during the nineteenth century A.D. has shed considerable light on this event. Schliemann found nine city layers on a site that closely matched Homer's description of the plains of Ilium. The seventh layer, a city which was burnt to the ground, flourished in the twelfth century B.C., a good four hundred years before Homer's day. It is this city that modern scholars deem to be the Troy of Homer's poems.

According to the *Iliad*, the Trojan War lasted a full ten years before culminating in the destruction of Troy. While it is unlikely that such a siege could have lasted so long (some scholars have suggested that the war lasted a mere ten days!), the event remained an important one to future generations. Some critics have suggested that the depiction of a unified Greece gave the poems a universal appeal. Note that for most of the history of ancient and classical Greece, the city-state or *polis* was the unit of government, not the nation as a whole. Thus, cities such as Sparta, Athens, and Thebes were ruled by isolated systems of government, although the many city-states shared in trade and culture. Wars between city-states were common, as was a tendency toward isolationism when the Greek peninsula was attacked by an outside foe.

What is remarkable about Homer's poems is not only that they depict a combined effort on the part of the Greek cities, but also do not favor one city exclusively over the others. Some scholars suggest that this is because Homer lived across the Aegean Sea in Asia Minor, and was therefore free to write without favoring his local community in the poem.

Homer's geographic separation from the Greek world would also explain why the Trojans, who would have been his neighbors in Asia Minor, were not depicted as ignorant barbarians but as figures equally as noble as their Greek enemies. Indeed, many modern readers find themselves admiring Hector, prince of Troy, far more than they do the often selfish and conceited Achilles.

The Genre of the Epic Poem

The epic poem is the most ancient form of literature, and Homer is considered the father of Western epic. He established most of the epic conventions which would be adopted by later writers of epic. History produced many poets who would walk in Homer's sandals, none more notable than the Roman poet, Virgil, whose *Aeneid* recounts the founding of Rome by Aeneas, one of the few survivors of Troy. Virgil's poem is considered a Secondary Epic, because it is a direct, written (not oral) imitation of Homer's own. The *Iliad* and the *Odyssey*, then, because they are the products of accumulative tradition and are not strictly imitative of an existent genre, are considered to be Primary Epics. But Virgil's greatness comes not only from his ability to imitate Homer, but from his ability to alter Homer's genre to suit his own contemporary needs.

Virgil's work would in turn have a profound effect upon the future of literature; this we note especially in Dante's medieval epic, the *Commedia*, which features Virgil himself as the protagonist's guide through the underworld. With the rise of Neoclassicism in the Renaissance, Tasso's *Gerusalemme Liberata* and Milton's *Paradise Lost* were also heavily influenced by Homer. This says nothing of the countless, lesser known epics written throughout the centuries based upon Homer's style, both in Greece, Rome, and Medieval and Renaissance Europe.

There are many conventions established by Homer that were subsequently developed over the centuries. What follows is a list of those epic conventions, not only as they appear in Homer, but how they are manifested over centuries of Homeric imitation:

(1) **Epic Hero**—The protagonist of an epic poem is a figure who unmistakably represents his nation, culture, or race. He must also be a figure of noble mien, considerable military prowess, and undying virtue.

(2) **Lengthy Narrative**—An epic poem must be a work of considerable length, spanning several books, cantos, or chapters.

(3) **Lofty Tone and Style**—The poem itself must assume a grave and serious tone. Although many epics contain lighter moments, these are always secondary to the primarily somber mood of the entire work. The poem must also be written in a grandiose, exalted style to distinguish it from works of lower orders.

(4) **Epic Similes**—The epic simile is an extended comparison between one element or character of the poem and some foreign entity. The simile is highly visual, and either forces the reader to consider the object of the simile

in a new light or helps reveal a secret about the element which would be too complex to detail didactically.

(5) **Catalogs/Genealogies**—An epic poem will often include copious inventories and catalogs of characters, equipment, or some other pertinent element of the plot. The poem will also supply expansive genealogies for important characters or artifacts, to lend an air of antiquity and authority to the respective element in the poem.

(6) **Supernatural Involvement**—The epic always features some form of divine intervention in the poem's main action. These other-worldly figures will either assist or antagonize the epic hero, although their involvement in matters will always be limited to some degree (i.e. they cannot dominate the entire narrative).

(7) **Invocation**—Most epic poems begin with an invocation to some higher power that the epic poet desires to guide his pen on his lofty undertaking. The poet often invokes the Muses, or a particular Muse (usually Calliope, the Muse of epic poetry). Other times, the poet might summon a particular deity or great power to lend inspiration to his endeavor. No matter the object of the request, the invocation serves as an introduction to the action that is about to unfold.

(8) *In Medias Res*—Many epics commence *in medias res,* or "in the midst of things." In other words, the narrative opens after a good deal of the important events of the epic have already transpired. As part of the convention, a character will recount the bypassed episodes later in the narrative, so that the reader may become familiar with the prehistory of the poem.

(9) **Voyage Across the Sea**—The epic hero and/or other characters will often journey across the sea to discover new lands or explore distant regions. The voyage serves to expand the setting of the drama considerably, and this helps to magnify the overall significance of the epic's action.

(10) **Trip to the Underworld**—A visit to the underworld is also a common epic motif. The epic hero will often gain intelligence from the departed spirits that he encounters. The journey both to and from the nether regions is most often fraught with peril.

(11) **Epic Battles**—Vivid descriptions of mighty battles, either one-on-one duels between universal champions or the amassed engagement of powerful armies, are a common feature of the epic poem. These mighty contests may indeed appear to glorify war, but they also personify the conflicts endured by the given nation, culture, or race that the epic hero symbolizes.

Master List of Characters

Achilles—*The greatest hero of the Greek forces at Troy; he discusses the fate of his son with Odysseus in the Underworld.*

Aegisthus—*The lover of Clytemnestra, Agamemnon's wife; he plans and executes Agamemnon's assassination.*

Aeolus—*The keeper of the Bag of Winds; he lends his charge to Odysseus to help him return home.*

Agelaus—*The suitor who leads his companions in the attack against Odysseus.*

Agamemnon—*The commander of the Greek forces at Troy; he discusses his death with Odysseus in the Underworld.*

Ajax Telamonius—*a Greek hero who committed suicide after Odysseus won Achilles' armor; he shuns Odysseus in the Underworld.*

Ajax Oïleus— *a Greek hero who committed the dreadful sin of wrenching Cassandra from the sanctuary of Athene's temple during the sack of Troy.*

Alcinoös—*The king of the Phaeaceans who entertains Odysseus.*

Amphimedon—*A suitor who later recounts his death and that of his companions to Agamemnon while in the Underworld.*

Amphinomus—*A chief suitor who is the least bent on violence, and who is vainly forewarned of danger by Odysseus.*

Anticleia—*Odysseus' mother, whom he meets in the Underworld.*

Antinoös—*A chief suitor who is the most arrogant and brazen of the pack; he and Eurymachus are the leaders of the suitors.*

Antiphates—*The king of the giant Laistrygones.*

Aphrodite—*Goddess of Love; she appears in Demodocus' story.*

Apollo—*God of Archery, Prophecy, and Poetry; he appears in Demodocus' story.*

Ares—*God of War; he appears in Demodocus' story.*

Arete—*The queen of the Phaeaceans and wife of Alcinoös.*

Argos—*Odysseus' aged dog.*

Athene—*Goddess of Wisdom and Battle, Odysseus' patron goddess and protector.*

Autolycus—*Odysseus' grandfather, who gave him his name.*

Calypso—*A nymph who imprisons Odysseus for seven years and takes him as a lover during that time.*

Cassandra—*The Prophetess of Apollo who is wrenched from Athene's temple by Ajax Oïleus and later killed alongside Agamemnon.*

Charybdis—*A creature that appears as a devouring whirlpool.*

Circe—*The goddess and sorceress who transforms Odysseus' shipmates into pigs, and later advises them on the proper course to return home.*

Clytemnestra—*The wife of Agamemnon who treacherously conspires against his life on his return from Troy.*

Demodocus—*The blind bard who entertains Odysseus and the Phaeaceans in the hall of Alcinoös.*

Dolius—*An old servant who remains loyal to Odysseus, but is the father of the wicked Melanthius.*

Eidothea—*The daughter of Proteus who assists Menelaus during his wanderings.*

Elpenor—*A companion of Odysseus whom he later meets in the Underworld.*

Eumaeus—*Odysseus' swineherd who remains loyal in his absence and cares for him while he is in disguise.*

Eupeithes—*The father of Antinoös who leads the suitors' relatives in the attack against Odysseus.*

Euryalus—*A Phaeacean athlete who insults Odysseus.*

Eurycleia—*The aged nurse of both Odysseus and Telemachus who remains loyal to them.*

Eurylochus—*Odysseus' secondary commander who leads the first expedition to Circe's cottage and escapes unharmed.*

Eurymachus—*A clever suitor with a quick tongue who gave the most gifts to win Penelope's hand.*

Eurynome—*The faithful maidservant of Penelope.*

Halitherses—*A prophetic Ithacan who predicts Odysseus' homecoming both when he leaves for Troy and in the year of his return.*

Helen—*The wife of Menelaus and daughter of Zeus; her departure with Paris began the Trojan War.*

Helius—*God of the Sun; his cattle are eaten by Odysseus' men.*

Hephaestus—*God of Blacksmiths; he traps the adulterous Aphrodite with her lover Ares during Demodocus' story.*

Hermes—*Messenger of the gods who tells Calypso to release Odysseus.*

Iros—*The beggar who sparred with Odysseus while he was in disguise.*

Laertes—*Father of Odysseus who retreats to his farm during his son's absence.*

Laodamas—*The son of Alcinoös who is among the greatest of the Phaeacean athletes.*

Leodes—*A prophetic suitor slain by Odysseus despite his appeal for mercy.*

Leukothea—*Sea goddess who aids Odysseus when he is in peril on his way from Calypso's island.*

Medon—*Herald of Odysseus who remains loyal to Penelope and Telemachus in his master's absence.*

Melanthius—*The wicked son of Dolius, a goatherd who abuses Odysseus while he is in disguise but sorely regrets it later.*

Menelaus—*King of Sparta and husband of Helen; he entertains Telemachus during his journey.*

Mentor—*The aged protector of Odysseus' property in his absence; his identity is often assumed by Athene.*

Nausikaa—*Princess of Scheria and daughter of Alcinoös; she meets Odysseus soon after his arrival on the island of Scheria.*

Neoptolemus—*The son of Achilles whose exploits are recounted to his deceased father by Odysseus in the Underworld.*

Nestor—*An aged counselor from the Trojan War; he entertains Telemachus during his journey.*

Odysseus—*The epic hero of the poem; his wanderings and home-coming are the subject of the narrative.*

Orestes—*The son of Agamemnon who avenges his father's death by slaying both his mother and Aegisthus.*

Peisistratus—*The son of Nestor who guides Telemachus to Menelaus' palace in Sparta.*

Penelope—*Odysseus' wife and mother of Telemachus; she stead-fastly awaits her husband's return.*

Peraeus—*A loyal friend of Telemachus.*

Phemius—*A bard who entertained the suitors unwillingly.*

Philoitius—*The loyal oxherd of Odysseus who joins him in his slaughter of the suitors.*

Polyphemus—*A wicked Cyclops and son of Poseidon who devours six of Odysseus' men, but is later blinded by his captives.*

Poseidon—*God of the Sea who harries Odysseus throughout his wanderings because of Odysseus' actions toward Polyphemus.*

Proteus—*The Old Man of the Sea who is imprisoned and interrogated by Menelaus during his wanderings.*

Scylla—*A monster who dwells opposite Charybdis that uses her six elongated necks to reach down and snatch six of Odysseus' men from his ship.*

Teiresias—*A prophet residing in the Underworld who advises Odysseus on his future course of action.*

Telemachus—*Odysseus' only son, who seeks out his missing father and later joins him in purging their household of the suitors.*

Theoclymenus—*A fugitive prophet who meets Telemachus on the shores of Pylus and accompanies him back to Ithaca.*

Zeus—*King of the gods, who appeases his daughter Athene when she wishes to rescue Odysseus from Poseidon's wrath.*

Summary of the Work

Odysseus, lord of the isle of Ithaca, has been missing from his kingdom for twenty years. The first ten had been spent fighting in the Trojan War, and the next ten had been spent in continual wanderings en route home from the war. His wife Penelope, in the meantime, has been harassed by dozens of suitors who have come from surrounding islands and Ithaca itself in order to win her hand in marriage. Penelope, desperately clinging to the hope that her husband is still alive, tries to stall the suitors by making them an idle promise: she will choose a husband from among them when she has finished weaving a burial shroud for her father-in-law, Laertes, who presently lives on a farm removed from the main city. However, when alone at night, Penelope secretly undoes the work of the shroud so that the fabrication of the garment will go on indefinitely. Unfortunately, the ruse has been discovered by the suitors, who now demand she choose one of them immediately.

The suitors, who have been awaiting her decision for several years, have in the meantime spent their days feasting in Odysseus' hall. In so doing, they are devouring his livestock and abusing his servants. The direct victim of their voracious behavior is Telemachus, the son of Odysseus who is now approaching manhood. Telemachus, who is the heir of Odysseus' property and title, is constantly derided and taunted by the suitors who waste his father's household.

Athene, goddess of wisdom and daughter of Zeus, begs her father to allow Odysseus to return home at last, for he has languished for seven years on the isle of the nymph Calypso, who holds him captive. Despite his brother Poseidon's hatred of Odysseus because of the fate of Polyphemus, Zeus yields to his daughter. Obtaining permission and aid from her father, Athene comes down from Mount Olympus to visit Telemachus in disguise. She convinces him that he should sail abroad and seek information concerning his father.

Though feeling hopeless concerning his father's fate, Telemachus agrees to the journey. Athene manages to get together a crew and ship for Telemachus, and he departs without informing his mother or the suitors. When his mother finds out, she despairs with the thought that Telemachus will share his father's fate. The suitors, angered at Telemachus' departure, sail out themselves to set an ambush for his return.

Telemachus arrives at Pylus with Athene, who is disguised as the elder friend of Odysseus, Mentor. There Telemachus is warmly received and entertained by the aged Nestor, the famous counselor of the Trojan War. Nestor informs Telemachus of the various ill-fated homecomings of the Greeks, especially the fate of Agamemnon, commander of the Greeks at Troy, who was slain by his wife, Clytemnestra, and her lover, Aegisthus. He then advises Telemachus to visit Menelaus, Agamemnon's brother, where he rules in Sparta. Borrowing a chariot from Nestor, Telemachus travels to Sparta with Peisistratus, Nestor's son.

Menelaus and his queen, Helen, whose retreat with Paris instigated the Trojan War, entertain Telemachus with splendor. Menelaus tells his guests of his own wanderings which resulted in his encounter with the Old Man of the Sea, Proteus. Capturing Proteus to obtain information concerning his own homecoming, Menelaus inadvertently discovered Odysseus' fate: namely, his imprisonment on Calypso's isle. Although unsure if Odysseus survived the intervening years, Menelaus is able to offer this information to Telemachus, who is still pessimistic concerning his father's fate.

Meanwhile, the god Hermes has been sent to Calypso's isle to demand Odysseus' liberation in Zeus's name. The nymph reluctantly agrees, and sends Odysseus on his way in a raft of his own making. However, Poseidon sees Odysseus' escape, and sends a storm to destroy him. With the help of Athene and the sea goddess, Leukothea, Odysseus is able to swim for several days and land exhausted on the isle of the Phaeaceans: Scheria. After having secured shelter for himself beneath a bush, Odysseus is wakened the next morning by the playful dancing of Nausikaa, Princess of the Phaeaceans, and the handmaids who accompany her to do the palace laundry. Odysseus and Nausikaa encounter each other, and the latter agrees to take him to the palace of her father, Alcinoös.

Odysseus, aided again by Athene, is welcomed warmly by Alcinoös and his queen, Arete. There is great feasting accompanied by the singing of the blind bard Demodocus, who recounts many of the Greek heroes' exploits in the Trojan War as well as narrating an amusing tale of the gods. There are also great games played in which Odysseus reluctantly takes part with great success. Having heard of Odysseus' journey from Calypso's isle, Alcinoös agrees to assist Odysseus with the Phaeaceans' magic ships, which can reach any destination in the world and return in a single day. However, Odysseus' hosts remain ignorant of his identity. When they learn he is the famous adventurer, Odysseus, they demand he tell them of his many adventures.

Odysseus begins his tale with the departure of his twelve ships from Troy and his early encounters with the Ciconians and Lotus-Eaters. He then recounts his adventure with Polyphemus the Cyclops. Having left most of his fleet at a different part of the Cyclopes' isle, Odysseus explored the strange land in his own vessel. He chose twelve men from his ship to join him in exploring the cavernous home of Polyphemus. However, when Polyphemus returned to his lair, he rolled a great stone over the entrance to his cave and proceeded to eat Odysseus' men two at a time, till only six remained with their leader. Odysseus tricked Polyphemus into drinking a potent wine unmixed with water, and while the giant Cyclops snored drunkenly, Odysseus and his men gouged out Polyphemus' eye with a wooden stake. Odysseus' cunning allowed them to escape the cave despite Polyphemus' attempts to block the cave entrance with his body. After his ship set out to sea to rejoin his fleet, he called to taunt Polyphemus, and the latter cursed him in his father Poseidon's name. This is how Odysseus incurred the enmity of this powerful deity.

Odysseus next borrowed from Aeolus the divine bag which sealed up the world's winds. However, Odysseus' greedy companions meant to seize some of their master's treasure, and unintentionally released all the winds at once. The fleet of ships was swept back to the island of Aeolus, who angrily banished the miserable Odysseus from his island. Odysseus' ships then met disaster in the land of the enormous Laistrygones. Caught by surprise, all his moored ships but his own personal vessel were speared by the giants and carried off. Odysseus' ship escaped alone. They arrived next on Circe's island, and half the party was sent ahead to explore a visible column of smoke. Eurylochus, Odysseus' second-in-command, led the men to Circe's cottage. The men entered at Circe's invitation, but Eurylochus himself refused to enter. Once inside, the men feasted with Circe, who transformed them into swine. Eurylochus escaped to inform Odysseus, who returned alone to face Circe. Aided by the herb moly bestowed on him by Hermes, Odysseus overcame Circe's sorceries and demanded his men's return. Circe complied, and was thereafter benevolent to Odysseus' party.

Circe entertained Odysseus' men for some time, then warned them that their journey could only continue after they had consulted the land of the dead. Though dreading the journey, Odysseus' men accompanied him on a voyage into the Underworld. Once there, Odysseus encountered the soul of the prophet Teiresias, who told him how to reach his home and informed him of the final journey he would make in years to come. Odysseus also saw the spirit of his mother, Anticlea, and the spirits of queens from many ages and lands. He also interviewed the souls of his deceased Greek comrades from the Trojan War, Agamemnon and Achilles. He finally witnessed the spirits of many dead spirits in torment, including Heracles, Tantalus, and Sisyphus.

Returning to Circe's island, Odysseus was given warning by the sorceress how to avoid the horrible fates associated with the Sirens' isle and the passage between Scylla and Charybdis. She also warned him to spare the cattle of Helius that reside on the island Thrinacea. Odysseus set out from Circe's isle, and his men plugged their ears versus the Sirens' singing, although Odysseus himself, tied to a mast, listened to their beguiling voices. His men then navigated the ship through the perilous cliffs inhabited by Scylla, a monstrous beast with six heads that reach down from towering heights, and Charybdis, a disastrous whirlpool. Avoiding Charybdis, the men were victimized by Scylla, who carried off six of their number before the ship was clear of the dangerous passage.

Odysseus' ship became stranded by storm winds on Thrinacea, despite Odysseus' hope to avoid this island. When their ship could not set out because of poor winds, the men broke down and devoured several of Helius' cattle. When the winds finally died down and the ship set sail, Helius coerced Zeus into punishing the ship. Zeus sent down a lightning bolt which destroyed the ship and all its crew except Odysseus, who floated off on a makeshift raft. He was carried all the way back to Charybdis, where he narrowly avoided death in the whirlpool. Odysseus finally came to be stranded on Calypso's island, and it is here that his tale ends.

The Phaeaceans are pleased with his tale. After they shower him with gifts that exceed the value of his lost treasure, Odysseus sets out in the magical ships of the Phaeaceans. While Odysseus himself sleeps peacefully on board, the Phaeaceans reach Ithaca in a matter of hours. Without waking him, the Phaeaceans disembark Odysseus and his goods. They return to Scheria, but are turned to stone by Poseidon when they are within sight of their harbor. Alcinoös recognizes the portent as the sign of an old prophecy at last fulfilled.

Odysseus awakens on Ithaca at last, but is unsure of his locale until he meets with Athene, who advises him concerning the situation in his kingdom and transforms him into the shape of an old beggar. Odysseus sets out and meets with Eumaeus the swineherd, who accepts Odysseus as a guest in his shelter and unwittingly reveals his loyalty to his master.

Telemachus begs his leave of Menelaus, and returns with

Peisistratus to Pylus. Before setting sail to Ithaca, Telemachus is joined by the fugitive prophet, Theoclymenus. Forewarned by Athene concerning the suitors' ambush, Telemachus avoids the trap and lands safely on shore. He sends his companions with the prophet on to the main city, while he himself, inspired by Athene, travels alone to Eumaeus' dwelling.

Telemachus meets his disguised father at the swineherd's shelter, and while Eumaeus is away informing Penelope of her son's return, Odysseus reveals himself to his overjoyed son; the two then commence hatching out a plan for the suitors' death.

After Eumaeus has returned, Telemachus returns to his household and the suitors, who have since abandoned their hope for ambushing their host. Shortly thereafter, Eumaeus and Odysseus head toward the main city. Along the way, they meet with the scurrilous Melanthius the goatherd, who rudely accosts Odysseus. Odysseus and Eumaeus arrive at last at Odysseus' palace, where Odysseus enters and begs from the suitors. While many of the suitors pity his appearance, some of them abuse him severely. Among those who abuse him most are the two leaders of the suitors, Antinoös and Eurymachos.

After the suitors return to their homes for the evening, Odysseus and Telemachus hide the armor and weapons that are normally kept in the main hall. Penelope then summons Odysseus in his beggar guise to her presence so that she may question him concerning his alleged claim to knowledge of her lost husband's whereabouts. During the interview, Penelope never suspects the beggar's identity. She is pleased by his talk of Odysseus, however, and orders the aged servant, Eurycleia, who nursed both Odysseus and Telemachus, to wash Odysseus' feet. While doing so, Eurycleia notices a scar on Odysseus' leg that he had received during a hunting incident while visiting the family of his maternal grandfather, Autolycus. Eurycleia almost reveals Odysseus' identity, but he quickly silences her.

The suitors arrive the next day, as do Eumaeus and Philoitius, an oxherd who has remained loyal to Odysseus. The suitors are soon gripped by a divinely sent, though temporary, hysteria. Theoclymenus, who has returned to the household, interprets this as a foreboding of doom. The fugitive prophet is ignored, however, so he leaves in despair. Penelope arrives bearing Odysseus' famous bow, which he did not carry with him to Troy, and proposes that the one suitor who can string it and shoot an arrow through twelve axe handles may marry her. Telemachus sets up the axe handles, and attempts to string the bow himself, but eventually fails. One by one the suitors attempt to string the bow but with no success.

It is at this point that Odysseus pulls Eumaeus and Philoitius into another room and reveals himself to them. Now part of his conspiracy, the two loyal thralls agree to bar the doors and prepare to arm themselves at the critical moment. Penelope is sent away, and Eumaeus brings Odysseus the bow, much to the disapproval of the suitors. Odysseus quickly strings the bow and shoots through the axe handles. He next takes an arrow and shoots Antinoös through the throat. He finally reveals himself to them fully, and begins picking them off one by one with his bow and arrows. Meanwhile, Telemachus, Eumaeus, and Philoitius arm themselves, and when Odysseus runs out of arrows, he does likewise. However, Melanthius the goatherd sneaks out of the room and starts bringing equipment to the remaining suitors. He is eventually stopped and bound by Eumaeus and Philoitius, who then rejoin Odysseus and Telemachus in the final battle against the suitors.

Odysseus and his allies overcome and slay all the suitors, then execute Melanthius and the bondswomen who were loyal to the suitors. The palace is cleaned of bloodshed, and Penelope is brought into Odysseus' presence. However, she refuses to believe that it is her husband until she craftily tricks him into revealing himself. She then embraces and accepts him, and they are reunited at last.

Meanwhile, the souls of the suitors arrive in the Underworld, and there Agamemnon asks them to relate the nature of their deaths. When he discovers that Odysseus has won back his home, the murdered general both rejoices and expresses envy at his friend's success. In the morning, Odysseus leaves the palace and visits his father, Laertes. After some delay, Odysseus reveals his identity to his rejoicing father, who brings him and his followers into his house. However, the families of the suitors, having performed the funeral rites for their dead, seek to avenge their kinsmen's deaths. They don armor and weaponry and march out to Laertes' farm. Odysseus and his companions ready themselves for battle, but the skirmish has only begun when Athene intervenes and stifles any bloodshed. Odysseus then reconciles himself with his enemies and reestablishes himself in the land.

Meter and Style in the Odyssey

The Greek text of the *Odyssey* as we have it is written predominantly in *Dactyllic Hexameter*: each line consists of six metrical feet, each of which consists of a stressed syllable followed by two unstressed syllables. By no means are dactyls used exclusively. In fact, the last foot of every line usually ends in either a spondee (two stressed syllables) or a troche (one stressed syllable followed by one unstressed syllable). Spondees frequently replace dactyls in other parts of certain lines as well.

Homer's style is famous for its flow and pacing. It is easy to follow and meant to be read briskly, unlike much modern poetry which is designed to be read carefully one line at a time. There are a wealth of details in descriptions, unlike other contemporary writings such as the Bible, which are reticent on all details but the most essential. Characterization is strong in Homer's writing; each character, large or small, is a distinctive individual with independent motivations. On the other hand, character development over the course of the narrative is minimal; characters are what they are and changes in personality are usually insignificant. Finally, one should not be surprised by the frequent use of formulaic repetition and contextually unseemly epithets, for Homer's narratives are the product of oral development, and these ingredients were essential to the spontaneous composition of oral poetry.

Estimated Reading Time

There are several excellent translations of the *Odyssey* in both poetry and prose; two of the most noted modern translations are those by Richmond Lattimore and Robert Fitzgerald. Each Book or chapter of the *Odyssey* can probably be read in an hour or two, so that a range of 25 to 50 hours span the average reading time of the poem as a whole.

The Odyssey

Book I

New Characters:

Poseidon: *god of the sea, enemy of Odysseus*

Zeus: *king of the gods*

Athene: *goddess of wisdom, Odysseus' patron*

Telemachus: *Odysseus' son*

Phemius: *bard forced to sing for the suitors*

Penelope: *Odysseus' wife, mother of Telemachus*

Antinoös: *leader and most brazen of the suitors*

Eurymachus: *crafty co-leader of the suitors*

Eurycleia: *aged maid who nursed both Odysseus and Telemachus*

Summary

    The narrator calls upon the Muse to help him narrate the story of Odysseus' wanderings and homecoming. We learn that he is imprisoned on Calypso's island, and that he is the victim of Poseidon's wrath.

    While Poseidon is away receiving a hecatomb, a massive sacrifice, from the Ethiopians, the gods sit in council on Mount Olympus. Zeus mourns the death of Agamemnon, the general who led the Greek forces at Troy, and rues the fact that Aegisthus,

Agamemnon's assassin, did not heed the gods' warning; now Aegisthus lies slain at the hand of Agamemnon's avenging son, Orestes. Athene reminds her father that Odysseus still languishes on Calypso's island due to Poseidon's wrath. Zeus agrees to send Hermes to command Calypso to release Odysseus; Athene herself plans to descend to Ithaca to stir Telemachus to seek out his father and thereby gain a reputation for himself.

Athene flies down to the palace of Odysseus and disguises herself as Mentes, a trader friend of Odysseus. She is greeted by Telemachus, who draws her away from the suitors who are wildly feasting in his hall. Telemachus explains to Mentes (Athene) that Odysseus is lost and his palace is besieged by voracious young men who waste his father's goods in his absence. They are suitors seeking the hand of Penelope, Odysseus' wife, who neither refuses nor accepts their suits.

Athene advises Telemachus to call an assembly to oust the suitors, and then suggests that he take a journey to Pylus and Sparta to seek news of his father. Athene then takes on the likeness of a bird and flies away; Telemachus recognizes her divinity and is emboldened by her visit. When Penelope descends to stifle the mournful singing of Phemius, which reminds her painfully of her missing Odysseus, Telemachus sends her away with the authority of master of the household. He then verbally abuses the suitors themselves, despite reproaches by the brazen Antinoös and sly Eurymachus.

The suitors finally leave for the evening, and Telemachus somberly retreats to his chamber. He is led by the nurse Eurycleia, who has been a member of the household since her purchase by Laertes, Odysseus' father, years ago. Telemachus then rests, brooding upon Athene's words and advice.

Analysis

At the beginning of Book I, we have the poem's invocation, one which countless other epics will mimic. The ingredients include the call upon a divine Muse to inspire the poet with the ability to perform a particular tale. The invocation also includes a very quick summary of the events which have transpired before the poem begins: the wanderings of Odysseus and his companions; the death of his friends for the sin of eating Helius' cattle; Odysseus' imprisonment on Calypso's isle; and the wrath of Poseidon which continually plagues the hero. This gives the poet's audience a sense of temporal perspective. They know now that the tale has begun *in medias res*, in the midst of things, and they can anticipate the eventual retelling of these events which they have missed (Books IX-XII).

Zeus's mention of Agamemnon's fate is a significant motif that constantly echoes Odysseus' situation throughout the narrative. The fates of Agamemnon, Clytemnestra, and Orestes are constantly likened and contrasted to those of Odysseus, Penelope, and Telemachus.[1] This is seen most clearly in Book I when Athene suggests to Telemachus:

> ... You should not go on
> clinging to your childhood. You are no longer of an age to do that.
> Or have you not heard what glory was won by great Orestes
> among all mankind, when he killed the murderer of his father,
> the treacherous Aigisthos, who had slain his famous father?
> So you too, dear friend, since I can see you are big and splendid,
> be bold also, so that in generations to come they will praise you.
> I. 296–302

So we see Athene spur Telemachus to action by comparing his paternal obligation to that of his young contemporary, Orestes.

Athene's disguise as Mentes also introduces a motif that runs throughout the narrative. There are constantly scenes of disguised identity followed by significant revelation; most of them are enacted by Odysseus himself. As Odysseus' patron, it is only fitting that Athene should perform the first example of this motif. Her revelation of divinity to Telemachus spurs him on to courage and determination, for before her arrival the young man had been lost in a state of timeless, inconclusive dreaming and fantasy about revenge, instead of taking pragmatic steps toward realizing that revenge.

---

1. This theory, which is often referred to throughout this study guide, is based upon a theory suggested by Richmond Lattimore in the introduction to his translation of the *Odyssey*.

Study Questions

1. Where is Odysseus located at the poem's commencement?

2. Which of the Olympian deities is his nemesis?

3. What did Odysseus do to inspire the god's wrath?

4. What is the correlation of family members between Agamemnon's family and Odysseus' household?

5. As whom does Athene disguise herself when she visits Telemachus?

6. Who are the chief suitors in Odysseus' house?

7. Why does Phemius' song disturb Penelope?

8. Who is Odysseus' father?

9. Where is he located during the time of Book I?

10. What is Eurycleia's association with both Odysseus and Telemachus?

Answers

1. Odysseus is on Calypso's island.

2. His nemesis is Poseidon.

3. He wounded Polyphemus, Poseidon's son.

4. The correlation is as follows: Agamemnon = Odysseus; Clytemnestra = Penelope; Orestes = Telemachus.

5. Athene disguises herself as Mentes.

6. The chief suitors are Antinoös and Eurymachus.

7. The song reminds her of Odysseus' own wanderings.

8. Odysseus' father is Laertes.

9. Laertes is on his farm removed from the main city.

10. Eurycleia was their nurse.

Suggested Essay Topic

Examine the various epithets that are constantly associated with the various characters: "thoughtful" Telemachus; "circumspect" Penelope; "resourceful," "enduring," and "godlike" Odysseus; and so on. What function do these epithets serve other than as formulaic constructions used in the oral poetic medium? How are these epithets appropriate to the characters associated with them? When are they not appropriate?

Book II

New Characters:

Mentor: *aged protector of Odysseus' property*

Halitherses: *prophetic Ithacan who predicts Odysseus' homecoming*

Summary

Telemachus arises in the morning and calls the people of Ithaca together for an assembly. This is the first time since Odysseus' departure for Troy that such a gathering has taken place. With a divine air of grace bestowed on him by Athene, Telemachus addresses the people, who are impressed by his speech. He demands that they take some action against the suitors and their outrages against his household and possessions.

Antinoös retorts that the cause of Telemachus' troubles lies not in the suitors but in Penelope herself, who keeps baiting the suitors with ungenuine promises of satisfaction. Furthermore, Penelope has kept the suitors off for three years by promising to marry one of them when she has completed the weaving of a burial shroud for her father-in-law, Laertes. The suitors have discovered that Penelope, hoping to stall the suitors indefinitely, undoes the work of the shroud every evening in order to make the work's completion impossible. Now they have forced her to finish the shroud and demand that she finally make the choice she promised she would make. Until she decides, Telemachus must suffer the suitors' presence in his household.

There are two outspoken advocates of Telemachus' cause at the assembly. The first is Halitherses, a prophet who predicted long ago that Odysseus would return home alone and disguised twenty years after his departure. During the council, two eagles fight each other wildly over the assembly; Halitherses augurs that this is a sign of doom for the suitors, who had best quit their actions now before it is too late. Eurymachus speaks up, however, and threatens the welfare of Halitherses and his family should the prophet continue to stir up trouble with his speech.

Telemachus' second advocate is Mentor, an aged friend of Odysseus who was charged with caring for Odysseus' personal matters while he was away. After Telemachus requests a ship

and crew to search for news of his father, Mentor supports him by blaming the Ithacans for their indifference to matters in Odysseus' household. However, he too is silenced by the angry suitors.

Matters end inconclusively, and the assembly is over abruptly. However, Athene, disguised as Mentor, stirs Telemachus to continue his plans for his journey. Telemachus returns home and, after dealing with the taunts of the suitors, descends to his storeroom and charges Eurycleia to prepare provisions for his journey. Despite her protests concerning the journey, Eurycleia obeys her master and even swears an oath of secrecy regarding the matter.

Meanwhile, disguised as Telemachus, Athene goes abroad and gathers a ship, crew, and gear for sailing. This done, she casts a spell that forces the suitors to sleep. It is a small matter, then, for Telemachus to bring the provisions down to the ship and sail off into the dead of night, with no one, not even Penelope, aware of his departure. Athene journeys with Telemachus, still disguised as Mentor.

Analysis

The epic council or assembly is another convention established through Homer's poetry. The *Iliad* had several important war meetings, and these are complemented by the more domestic assembly found in Book II of the *Odyssey*. As was the case in the *Iliad*, speakers arise and state their positions in a somewhat orderly fashion, arguing point for point until a solution is reached. The fact that the Ithacans are unable to come to a solid conclusion is a sign of their weakness and indecisiveness. Many of those present sympathize with Telemachus, but feel defenseless against the vigorous suitors.

We are given an interesting picture of Penelope for the second time since the poem began. Once more, we find that she is no innocent and naive wretch forced from the beginning to marry against her will. In Book II, we receive the second indication that she has been enticing the suitors with promises of marriage from the very beginning. Despite Antinoös' brash, insulting manner, we can almost sympathize with his appeal to understand the suitors' position: Penelope has promised to marry one of them, and they have doled out a good deal of wealth in presents in order to achieve her favor. Were they to end their suit prematurely, they would lose a good deal of money and time better spent elsewhere. Later in the poem, we get a further indication of just how much money has been invested in the endeavor. Eurymachus, in fact, has given Penelope's father quite a handsome supply of presents, and leads the others in wealth bestowed to gain her family's favor.

Penelope is a figure of guile and resourcefulness much like her husband, and Odysseus himself will admire her ability to amass gifts from the suitors later on when he returns. It is important, then, for us to realize this very interesting and conniving side of Penelope's character.

Study Questions

1. What are the two reasons that Telemachus calls the Ithacans to assembly?

2. Who are Telemachus' outspoken advocates in the assembly?

3. What is the chief means employed by Penelope in order to stall the suitors?

4. What is the sign read by Halitherses during the assembly?

5. How does Halitherses interpret the sign?

6. What personae are assumed by Athene in Book II?

7. How does Telemachus manage to acquire a ship and crew?

8. Why does Eurycleia protest against Telemachus' proposed journey?

9. What promise does he exact from her?

10. What ritual do the sailors perform once the ship has taken to the sea?

Answers

1. He wants them to remove the suitors from his home, and he wants them to supply him a ship for his voyage.

2. His two advocates are Mentor and Halitherses

3. She stalls them by undoing the work of Laertes' shroud.

4. Two eagles battle overhead.

5. He interprets this to mean that the suitors are in danger from a returning Odysseus.

6. She becomes both Mentor and Telemachus on separate occasions.

7. Athene gathers them together for him.

8. She does not want him to share his father's fate.

9. She will not announce his departure.

10. They pour a libation to Athene to protect them on their journey.

Suggested Essay Topic

Examine the arguments made by each speaker at the Ithacan assembly. How do the characters' speeches reflect their individual personalities? Analyze both what the characters say and the manner and mood in which they say it. How do the styles and rhetorical strategies employed by the various speakers compare and contrast with one another? How are these similarities and differences significant? What conclusions can we draw about the speakers' character traits as depicted in their speech?

Book III

New Characters:

Nestor: *the aged counselor of the Greeks during the Trojan War*

Peisistratus: *the youngest son of Nestor*

Summary

Telemachus' ship arrives safely on the Greek mainland at the city of Pylus. This is the domain of Nestor, the aged counselor of the Greek forces at Troy; he is renowned for his wisdom and strategy. The Pylians are in the midst of celebrating a feast dedicated to Poseidon, the Earthshaker. Seeing Telemachus and Athene (still disguised as Mentor) approaching from the shore, Nestor's sons greet them heartily and invite them to the feast. Foremost among the sons in greeting the new arrivals is Peisistratus, Nestor's youngest son who is close in age to Telemachus.

After the meal is finished, Telemachus explains his journey to Nestor, who is more than willing to swap endless stories with the son of his dear friend, Odysseus. Nestor informs Telemachus that while Odysseus had begun to accompany Menelaus and him when they departed from Troy, Odysseus later turned back to perform sacrifices with Agamemnon, who had remained at Troy for that purpose. Nestor, the great warrior Diomedes, and Menelaus had remained together on their journey home.

Telemachus questions Nestor concerning Agamemnon's assassination and Menelaus' conspicuous absence during such an event. Nestor explains that Menelaus' ships were scattered by storm winds, and that half his fleet drifted to Egypt and to other faraway lands beyond the sea. Meanwhile, Aegisthus, who had not gone to the war, remained behind in Mycenae to seduce Clytemnestra, Agamemnon's wife. Having slain Agamemnon, Aegisthus ruled Mycenae for seven years before being cut down by Agamemnon's son, Orestes. It was while Orestes was burying his hated mother and her lover that Menelaus returned home in the eighth year of his wanderings.

Because Menelaus had traveled the world for so long, Nestor suggests that Telemachus visit the Spartan king in the hope that he has heard some news concerning Odysseus. Nestor has just invited Telemachus to stay the night in his palace when Athene chooses to depart from them, revealing her divinity by transforming herself into a vulture.

Nestor, overjoyed that Athene has chosen to favor Telemachus as she has the man's father, feels an overwhelming sense of honor at her visitation. The next morning, he and his family perform a ritual sacrifice to Athene. Afterwards, Nestor's children prepare a chariot and horses for Telemachus to visit Sparta. Peisistratus accompanies Telemachus on his journey, and the new companions ride for two days toward Menelaus' kingdom.

Analysis

Critics have used Nestor as a prime example of the unity of Homer's poems. Just as he was in the *Iliad*, so too is the Nestor of the *Odyssey* inclined to tell old stories and speak verbosely. Nestor serves in many other ways as a bridge between the two Homeric poems. For example, he mentions the strong relationship between Athene and Odysseus at Troy. The old man notes that he

> . . . never saw the gods showing such open affection
> as Pallas Athene, the way she stood beside him, openly;
> if she would deign to love you as she did him, and care for you
> in her heart, then some of those people might forget about mar-
> rying.
>
> III. 221–224

We know, of course, that Athene does indeed care for Telemachus in a manner approximating her affection for Odysseus; ironically enough, she is right there disguised as Mentor.

Yet while the passage serves to link the fates of father and son, it also serves to separate them as well. While Telemachus has been visited twice now by Athene in disguise, the goddess used to display "open affection" for Odysseus and stand "beside him, openly." In other words, she honored this mortal in a way few immortals dared: she appeared to him undisguised. Of course, she will disguise herself often before Odysseus during the course of the *Odyssey*, but this, she explains, is due to her fear of Poseidon's wrath. When Odysseus returns to Ithaca, she will again resume that unique relationship of openness she shares only with this lone mortal.

Nestor also continues the symbolic link of the Atreus House with Odysseus' family. After describing Orestes' act of vengeance against Aegisthus, Nestor remarks to Telemachus: "So you too, dear friend, for I see you are tall and splendid, / be brave too, so that men unborn may speak well of you" (III. 199–200). And Athene herself (as Mentor) asserts that

> I myself would rather first have gone through many hardships
> and then come home, and look upon my day of returning,
> than come home and be killed at my own hearth, as Agamemnon
> was killed, by the treacherous plot of his wife, and by Aigisthos.
>
> III. 232–35

In this way, Agamemnon's speedy but fatal homecoming is contrasted with Odysseus' tedious but successful return. Here, Homer further explores these two houses and their contrasting fates.

Study Questions

1. What is the name of the first kingdom visited by Telemachus on his travels?

2. What is Nestor's family celebrating when Telemachus arrives at their city?

3. Which son of Nestor befriends and accompanies Telemachus on his journey?

4. When did Nestor and Odysseus part company?

5. Where was Menelaus when Agamemnon was assassinated?

6. What activity was Orestes engaged in when Menelaus finally returned to Greece?

7. Whom does Nestor suggest Telemachus visit?

8. In what manner does Athene take her leave of Telemachus and Nestor?

9. How does Nestor react toward her departure?

10. What occurs in the morning before Telemachus continues on his journey?

Answers

1. The first kingdom Telemachus visits is Pylus.

2. They are celebrating a feast for Poseidon.

3. Peisistratus befriends and accompanies Telemachus.

4. Odysseus turned his ships back toward Troy to console Agamemnon.

5. He was still wandering in his ships.

6. He was burying Clytemnestra and Aegisthus.

7. He suggests that Telemachus visit Menelaus.

8. She turns into a vulture.

9. He rejoices, proud of her visitation.

10. Nestor's people sacrifice to Athene.

Suggested Essay Topic

Examine Nestor's personality and character. What distinguishes him from other characters who serve as storytellers during the course of the narrative? What distinguishing features mark his speech? What is the general impression of his character that is given in the *Odyssey*? What means does Homer employ in order to achieve this impression?

Book IV

New Characters:

Menelaus: *the king of Sparta*

Helen: *his wife, instigator of the Trojan War*

Eidothea: *daughter of Proteus*

Proteus: *sea god interrogated by Menelaus during his travels*

Ajax Oïleus: *blasphemous Greek who pulled Cassandra from Athene's temple*

Medon: *a herald who remains loyal to Penelope and Telemachus*

Summary

Telemachus and Peisistratus arrive in Sparta and enter Menelaus' palace. They are warmly received during a wedding celebration in honor of Menelaus' two children. Megapenthes, the king's son through a bondswoman, is about to marry a Spartan woman, and Hermione, the only child of Helen, is being sent to marry Neoptolemus, the son of Achilles. The two travelers feast with Menelaus, who, though unaware of their identities, begins to muse about his sorrows during the Trojan War. He even mentions his grief concerning the lost Odysseus, at which Telemachus weeps. Helen enters and guesses Telemachus' identity immediately. The four of them begin reminiscing about Troy, and weep for those that died there until Peisistratus begs them to cease their sorrow.

Helen, however, cheers everyone up by drugging the wine with an ingredient she discovered in Egypt that brings happiness to all who partake of it. Afterwards, she recounts a story of Odysseus in Troy. Disguised as a beggar during a spying mission, Odysseus was discovered by Helen, who promised not to reveal his identity until he returned to the Greek camp safely. Having acquired a good body of intelligence, Odysseus fled to the Greek camp, but not before he first slaughtered several.

Menelaus then recalls the time when Odysseus and many of the Greek soldiers were hiding in the Trojan Horse. Helen had come to mischievously tempt the hidden Greeks by calling to them with the voices of their respective wives. It was only through Odysseus'

steadfast spirit and commanding force that the Greeks who suc-
cumbed to her trap were silenced until the danger was over.

The guests are finally led to their bedchambers, but in the
morning Menelaus returns to interview Telemachus, who informs
the Spartan king of his purpose there and the troubles besieging
his household. Menelaus recounts for Telemachus a story of his
own wanderings. After leaving Egypt, Menelaus' ships became
stranded on an island because of poor winds. When his men were
on the verge of starvation, a nymph named Eidothea, the daughter of the sea god Proteus, took pity on Menelaus. She told him
that her father Proteus, if captured, could advise Menelaus on how
to achieve his homecoming. In the morning, Eidothea skinned four
seals, and used the hides to conceal Menelaus and three companions on the seashore. When Proteus came up to the beach to take

a nap with his seals, Menelaus and his men sprang upon him and held him tightly. Proteus tried to escape by transforming himself into various beasts and natural forces, such as water and magical fire. Menelaus held tightly, and when Proteus surrendered at last, he told Menelaus what he wished to know: the Spartan had rendered insufficient sacrifices to the gods; he must therefore return to Egypt to make restitution before being able to return home.

At Menelaus' request, Proteus also narrated the death of Ajax Oïleus, whose ships were destroyed by Poseidon at Athene's behest; it was this Ajax who had pulled Cassandra unwillingly from Athene's temple. Ajax almost escaped destruction by climbing upon a sea crag, but arrogantly claimed his escape was a sign of his superiority over the gods; Poseidon, enraged, pulled him down to a watery death. Proteus also recounted Aegisthus' ambush of Agamemnon, which occurred during a pretended festival; Menelaus wept to hear of his brother's death. Finally, Proteus told Menelaus of Odysseus, who was imprisoned at that time on Calypso's isle. Menelaus finally tells of his journey back to Egypt, his sacrifices there, and eventual return home. Here, Menelaus' stories end.

Although unsure if his father has survived since the time of Proteus' tale, Telemachus has some notion now of his father's fate. Despite Menelaus' desire to detain him in Sparta, Telemachus expresses his earnest wish to return home.

Meanwhile, the suitors finally learn of Telemachus' voyage. Angered at his defiance, Antinoös induces the others to plot against Telemachus' life. They plan to ambush him on his return home as he passes through a narrow channel separating Ithaca from the isle of Samos. Medon the herald, who learns of their plot, rushes to tell Penelope, who also knew nothing of Telemachus' journey. She desperately anticipates disaster, until Eurycleia convinces her that she should pray to Athene to receive comfort. Penelope complies, and Athene answers her prayer by soothing her fears in a dream.

Analysis

The storytelling motif runs strongly through these scenes at Sparta. What is interesting about the stories is the hidden messages that are consciously conveyed from the storytellers to their audience. For example, Helen's story about her loyalty to Odysseus during his brief stay at Troy is meant to convey several messages. She makes it clear to Telemachus that she was fond of his father. She also suggests to all of those present that, despite her guilt in the entire affair, she was part of the war effort in favor of the Greeks in her own small way. She is certainly aware of their curiosity concerning her motivation for adultery. She therefore adds the detail of the women's lament about the slain Trojans, with the following addition:

> . . . but my heart
> was happy, my heart had changed by now and was for going back
> home again, and I grieved for the madness that Aphrodite
> bestowed when she led me there away from my own dear country,
> forsaking my own daughter, my bedchamber, and my husband,
> a man who lacked no endowment either of brains or beauty.
>
> IV. 259–264

Her marital disloyalty was on account of a "madness that Aphrodite bestowed" upon her, not from any voluntary decision on her part. The image she has presented of herself is that of the captured prisoner, struggling to aid her rescuers in any way that she can.

It is only appropriate that Menelaus, who must still nurse a grudge somewhere in his soul for the wife who caused him so much grief and pain, change this image of his wife with his own story. He presents a story that does not depict Helen as being helpful to the Greeks, but as being a terrible hindrance to them. Although he admits that she had "been moved by / some divine spirit who wished to grant glory to the Trojans" (IV. 274–75), we cannot help but notice the jab at her integrity inherent in the story. The matter was so dire, he adds, that Odysseus had "saved the lives of all the Achaians / until such time as Pallas Athene led you [Helen] off from us" (IV. 288–89). Helen's threat was not only one that endangered the Greek heroes' plans, but also one that imperiled their lives. This threat to his father, Odysseus, could not have been missed by Telemachus, as Menelaus perhaps intended it.

Another noteworthy feature of Helen's speech is the foreshadowing that Homer has worked into it concerning Odysseus. We note that he enters the city of Troy disguised as a beggar in order to gain information and slay some of his enemies. Odysseus will do likewise toward the end of the poem, when he enters his own house disguised as a beggar in order to ascertain the loyalty of his household members and to murder those who have betrayed him.

Study Questions

1. What is the festive occasion in Menelaus' palace when Telemachus arrives?

2. Who is the first to recognize Telemachus in Sparta?

3. Why does Peisistratus wish the weeping to end?

4. How does Helen stop everyone's sorrow?

5. What foreshadowing takes place in Helen's story?

6. How is Helen presented in Menelaus' tale of the Trojan Horse?

7. How does Menelaus know of Odysseus' fate?

8. How did Menelaus learn how to capture Proteus?

9. Why doesn't Telemachus accept Menelaus' gift of horses?

10. How do the suitors react when they learn of Telemachus' voyage?

Answers

1. The occasion is the weddings of Megapenthes and Hermione.

2. Helen is the first to recognize Telemachus.

3. He is reminded of his deceased brother, Antilochus.

4. She uses a drug she obtained in Egypt.

5. Helen depicts Odysseus as a spy disguised as a beggar.

6. She is helping the Trojans against the Greek warriors, including Odysseus.

7. He captured and interrogated the knowledgeable sea god, Proteus.

8. He was informed by Proteus' daughter, Eidothea.

9. Ithaca is not conducive to the breeding of horses.

10. They are angry and vengeful.

Suggested Essay Topic

Scholars have dubbed the first four books of the *Odyssey* as the "Telemachy," for the books deal almost exclusively with the journeys of Telemachus. In what ways are these books an appropriate introduction to Homer's work? In what ways are the books an inappropriate introduction? Note the many references to Odysseus in these books. What picture do we have of him before he even walks onto the stage in Book V? Is our view of him negative or positive? How does the picture we have of him coincide with the later Odysseus who appears in the poem?

Book V

New Characters:

Hermes: *the messenger of Zeus*

Calypso: *nymph who holds Odysseus captive for seven years*

Odysseus: *the epic hero of the narrative*

Leukothea: *sea goddess who aids Odysseus in his plight*

Summary

At a council of the gods, Athene renews her suit to Zeus to free Odysseus from Calypso's isle. Zeus complies, and sends Hermes on his way to break the news to Calypso. Hermes descends to earth from Mount Olympus, and alights on Calypso's isle. There, he tells the beautiful goddess that Zeus wills her to release Odysseus. Though distraught and angry over Zeus's decree, Calypso obeys. After Hermes has departed, the goddess searches for Odysseus, and

finds him weeping upon the shore, staring out upon the barren waters.

Calypso tells Odysseus of the gods' will, and though he initially suspects a trick, Odysseus welcomes the news. Calypso offers him immortality if he should choose to remain with her, but Odysseus refuses, longing only for his wife and home. The next day, supplied with carpenter's tools from Calypso, Odysseus begins making a large raft for himself, one with a sail and tackle capable of making a great journey. Calypso provides him with food, water, and wine, and fills his sails with a strong following wind.

Odysseus departs from the island and sails for seventeen days before sighting Scheria, the isle of the Phaeaceans. Poseidon, returning from Ethiopia, notes Odysseus' escape and decides to harass him a bit more. He unleashes the fury of the storm clouds, and sweeps the tiny vessel with all four of the world's mighty winds. Odysseus despairs, wishing he had died in Troy rather than suffer such an ignoble fate. A wave tears him out of the raft, although he is eventually able to surface and regain the raft.

The sea goddess Leukothea, once the mortal Ino, pities Odysseus. She advises him to abandon both the raft and the weighty clothing that Calypso had given him as a parting gift. She also bestows upon him a magic veil that, if tied about his body, would give him the stamina he needs to swim to Scheria. Odysseus chooses to wait until the raft is destroyed, then he abandons his clothing, ties the veil around his body, and begins swimming. Meanwhile, Poseidon, satisfied with his mischief, leaves the scene. Athene arrives and stills all the winds but the North Wind. Odysseus is carried toward Scheria for two days until, on the third, he comes very close to the shore.

Unfortunately, there are rough breakers at the edge of the island, and a sheer cliff beyond them. While Odysseus is pondering his next move, a wave carries him toward the cliff, but Athene gives him the notion to grab the rocks in order to resist the water's pull toward the cliff face. The backwash of the wave, however, pulls him again out to sea. Climbing to the surface of the water once more, Odysseus swims around the island until he sees a river outlet within accessible range. After intoning a hurried prayer to the river, Odysseus swims into the river safely. He crawls upon the shore and collapses in complete exhaustion. He then rises, and tosses the veil back into the river stream, as Leukothea had commanded, and the sea goddess retrieves her magic cloth.

Fearing that he might freeze to death on the windy riverbank, Odysseus ascends to a wood, where he buries himself in a pile of leaves beneath two dense bushes. Athene then lulls him to sleep so that he might recover from his trials.

Analysis

Here we meet Odysseus at last, and we are given many examples of his steadfast spirit and endurance. His willingness to retain his mortality and withstand the many dangers that lie ahead of him endears Odysseus' character to his audience. There is always a hollow mockery in Homer's depictions of the gods' antics, and we are most always interested in the deeds of men, not immortals. Therefore, as scholars have pointed out, Odysseus' rejection of Calypso's offer may keep him in danger, but it also keeps him part of the dynamic world of heroism, and frees him from the static, listless world of the gods.

Calypso's reason, though divine, is naive because of its very arrogance. She assumes that Odysseus will remain with her because her beauty is greater and longer lasting than Penelope's. She cannot perceive the internal beauty that one mortal may perceive in another. We see Odysseus' spirit and character summed up so well in the following passage:

> Goddess and queen, do not be angry with me. I myself know
> that all you say is true and that circumspect Penelope
> can never match the impression you make for beauty and stature.
> She is mortal after all, and you are immortal and ageless.
> But even so, what I want and all my days I pine for
> is to go back to my house and see my day of homecoming.
> And if some god batters me far out on the wine-blue water,
> I will endure it, keeping a stubborn spirit inside me,
> for already I have suffered much and done much hard work
> on the waves and in the fighting. So let this adventure follow.
>   V. 215–224

Here we see summed up Odysseus' unbreakable will and desire to struggle on as a mortal until he reaches the home he so desperately longs for.

Now that Odysseus' adventures have begun to be related in the main narrative action, there are more epic similes in this book than there have been in the four preceding books combined. While the epic similes in the *Odyssey* are generally inferior to and less frequent than those found in the *Iliad*, there are some that offer crisp images that have a powerful effect on the surrounding narrative. Critics have noted the effects of many of the epic similes: the pebbles clinging to the octopus' tentacles give us a vivid, negative impression of the skin being torn from Odysseus' fingers (432–35); the smoldering log buried in ashes to preserve its hidden spark of fire gives us a clear perception of Odysseus' flickering spark of life being tenderly preserved in the bed of leaves (488–91). Perhaps the most touching simile of all is that which we find in lines 394–399:

And as welcome as the show of life again in a father
is to his children, when he has lain sick, suffering strong pains,
and wasting long away, and the hateful death spirit has brushed
    him,
but then, and it is welcome, the gods set him free of his sickness,
so welcome appeared land and forest now to Odysseus,
and he swam, pressing on, so as to set foot on the mainland.

Here we see how fleeting and desperate is the hope that Odysseus
has nourished concerning his arrival at a safe port; so fleeting and
desperate is the hope of children whose father's health hangs pre-
cariously between life and death.

Study Questions

1. Who informs Calypso of Zeus's will?

2. What is Calypso's reaction to this information?

3. What is Odysseus' usual activity during the day on Calypso's
island?

4. What gift does Calypso offer Odysseus to convince him to
remain with her?

5. How else does she seek to dissuade him from his journey?

6. By what means does Odysseus leave the island?

7. What causes the storm winds to descend upon Odysseus?

8. What gods aid him in his distress at sea?

9. What island does he land upon?

10. What is the name of the people who reside there?

Answers

1. Hermes informs Calypso of Zeus's will.

2. She is sad but obedient.

3. He weeps on the shore of the sea.

4. Calypso offers Odysseus immortality.

5. She warns him of the many dangers still awaiting him.

6.   Odysseus leaves on a raft of his own making.

7.   The storm winds are the result of Poseidon's wrath.

8.   Odysseus is aided by Leukothea and Athene.

9.   Odysseus lands on the island of Scheria.

10.   The inhabitants of Scheria are the Phaeaceans.

Suggested Essay Topic

Examine several of the epic similes found in this and other books of the *Odyssey*. Identify each element in the simile and its relation to elements (characters, events, objects, etc.) in the narrative proper. What emotions, moods, and other factors can we elicit from the epic simile that were not present in the direct description of the element itself? Are these new feelings appropriate to the events that surround the simile? Does the simile enhance the narrative or distract us from it?

Book VI

New Characters:

Nausikaa: *princess of the Phaeaceans who greets Odysseus on Scheria*

Alcinoös: *king of the Phaeaceans*

Arete: *queen of the Phaeaceans*

Summary

While Odysseus sleeps peacefully out in the wilderness of Scheria, Athene appears to Nausikaa, princess of the Phaeaceans and daughter of King Alcinoös, in a dream vision. Disguised as one of Nausikaa's young friends, Athene suggests that Nausikaa be a dutiful daughter and potential wife, and go to wash the palace laundry. Upon awakening, Nausikaa requests a mule-drawn cart from her father, who allows her to bring the wash down to the river with some of her attendants.

The princess travels to the river, and there she and her maidservants wash the laundry and leave it out to dry in the sun. They next begin dancing and passing a ball to one another. During their game, the girls let out a tremendous cry that awakens Odysseus, who has been slumbering nearby. Hiding his private parts with some stray foliage, Odysseus appears before the young ladies. Startled by his entrance and bedraggled appearance, the girls flee in all directions. However, Nausikaa stands her ground and converses with Odysseus.

Odysseus, deciding that it would be better for him to supplicate Nausikaa from a distance rather than approach her and grasp her knees, begs her for her aid. Nausikaa grants his request, allows him to bathe and anoint himself, and then lends him some clothing. He now has the appearance of a god, thanks to some help from Athene, and Nausikaa's entourage is impressed. They feed the famished adventurer and agree to take him to the city.

However, fearing that gossipers might misconstrue the situa-

tion, Nausikaa leaves Odysseus out in Alcinoös' grove, and tells him to enter the city only after the girls have had sufficient time to reach the palace themselves. Alone in the orchard, Odysseus prays to Athene to help his supplication before the Phaeaceans succeed.

Analysis

Book VI contains an element which, although not scarce in the *Odyssey*, is certainly very rare in most epic poems: comedy. The comic element is unmistakable in these scenes. Odysseus' embarrassment when making his approach to the girls and right before bathing, as well as the girls' terrified reactions to his nakedness, cannot help but elicit a lighter mood in the poem's action, which until now had centered solely on the horrible problems faced by Odysseus and his family.

Even the epic similes, so solemn and grave in Book V, must appear humorous in this setting:

> So speaking, great Odysseus came from under his thicket,
> and from the dense foliage with his heavy hand he broke off
> a leafy branch to cover his body and hide the male parts,
> and went in the confidence of his strength, like some hill-kept lion,
> who advances, though he is rained on and blown by the wind, and both eyes
> kindle; he goes out after cattle or sheep, or it may be
> deer in the wilderness, and his belly is urgent upon him
> to get inside of a close steading and go for the sheepflocks.
> So Odysseus was ready to face young girls with well-ordered
> hair, naked though he was, for the need was on him . . .
>
>   VI. 127–136

Here, the ravenous lion, buffeted by the elements but striving onward to sate his all-consuming hunger on helpless sheep, is compared to the salt-covered Odysseus, ragged from days at sea, and filled with a hunger of an entirely different nature. The relation of the sheep to the girls can be seen clearly in retrospect when the girls flee before this ominous figure of male sexuality as sheep would flee before a hungry lion. This simile does not serve merely to make us once again pity the poor, travel-beaten Odysseus; it is rather an attempt to lighten the tension filling much of the first five books.

Study Questions

1. Who were the Phaeaceans' former neighbors?
2. Why does Nausikaa decide to wash the palace laundry?
3. What is she too embarrassed to mention to her father?
4. What is unique about the dance performed by the Phaeacean women?
5. How is Odysseus awakened?
6. What is the handmaidens' reaction to his appearance?
7. What is Nausikaa's reaction to his appearance?
8. What decision must Odysseus make concerning his approach to Nausikaa?
9. What is the main reason that Odysseus appears godlike to the Phaeacean ladies?
10. Why is Nausikaa afraid to bring Odysseus into the city with her?

Answers

1. The Phaeaceans' former neighbors were the Cyclopes.
2. Athene inspires her to do it.
3. She is embarrassed to tell her father her desire for marriage
4. The Phaeacean women toss a ball back and forth while they dance.
5. The girls scream in excitement when the ball goes astray.
6. They flee in terror.
7. Nausikaa stands her ground.
8. He must decide whether to keep his distance or approach her and grasp her knees in supplication.
9. Athene enhances his appearance.
10. It might appear scandalous to some of the Phaeaceans.

Suggested Essay Topic

Compare the various comic aspects of Book VI with parallel passages in the poem of a more serious nature. Look, for example, at Odysseus' decision-making, Athene's enhancement of beauty, and epic similes. How is the mocking of previous conventions more effective than simply inventing new narrative techniques for comic action?

Book VII

Summary

Nausikaa returns to the palace, where a maid prepares her a meal. Odysseus himself eventually heads toward the city and is greeted by Athene, who is disguised as a young girl. Athene offers to guide Odysseus to the palace of Alcinoös. In order to avoid rude inquiry, she forms a magical mist around Odysseus which renders him invisible to his surroundings. Leading him to the palace, Athene tells Odysseus that he will be accepted by the Phaeaceans if he is able to win the favor of the queen, Arete, whose people love her well. Athene then departs from Scheria, and journeys to Athens.

Odysseus admires Alcinoös' splendid palace, which is worked in finely wrought gold and silver both within and without. There is an orchard outside the courtyard which contains all manner of fruit as well as a vineyard; the fruit stays in season all year round. Entering the palace, Odysseus heads straight for Arete. He grasps her knees in supplication, and as he does so, the mist departs from him. The Phaeaceans are startled by his sudden appearance, but they are impressed by his speech requesting conveyance home.

Alcinoös allows Odysseus to join in their feasting, after which he promises the stranger the use of his magic ships, which can reach any worldly destination and return in a single day. Arete notices the Phaeacean clothing worn by Odysseus, and questions him accordingly. The long-suffering hero sums up for them his shipwreck on Calypso's isle, his seven years' detainment there, his calamitous voyage to Scheria, and finally his warm reception by

Nausikaa, who lent him the clothing. Alcinoös hints at a marriage between Odysseus and his daughter, who has scorned all other suitors. Odysseus, however, clearly displays his desire to return home. Arete has her servants prepare a bed for Odysseus, and the weary adventurer retires for the evening.

Analysis

In Book VII, we see the epitome of a motif that runs throughout the *Odyssey*: the relationship of host to guest. We saw the kind treatment Telemachus bestowed on Athene when she was disguised as Mentes as well as the great hospitality extended to Telemachus by both Nestor and Menelaus. Now it is Odysseus himself who comes as a stranger to a foreign court and must act accordingly. Indeed, the role of foreign visitor is one which Odysseus knows well, for he has wandered long and far and knows the customary courtesies expected of guests. Contrasted with his seasoned guest, Alcinoös, although kind and benevolent as a host, is unused to receiving guests, and is initially unsure of how to react to Odysseus' suit. After Odysseus has humbled himself by sitting in a heap of ashes, no one, including Alcinoös, knows quite how to react. Finally, an elder named Echeneus, the oldest man of Scheria, speaks:

> Alkinoös, this is not the better way, nor is it fitting
>   that the stranger should sit on the ground beside the hearth, in
>   the ashes.
> These others are holding back because they await your order.
> But come, raise the stranger up . . .

> VII. 159–162

Echeneus tactfully reminds Alcinoös of his duties as a host to a stranger. Once again, it is not Alcinoös' social grace and magnanimity that is lacking; it is his inexperience with situations of this sort that temporarily holds him back from action.

We are also given insight into another motif of the poem: the nature of divine disguise. Alcinoös suggests that Odysseus might be a god who has come to test the Phaeaceans' benevolence toward guests:

> But if he is one of the immortals come down from heaven,
> then this is a new kind of thing the gods are devising;
> for always in time past the gods have shown themselves clearly
> to us, when we render them glorious grand sacrifices,
> and they sit beside us and feast with us in the place where we do,
> or if one comes alone and encounters us, as a wayfarer,
> then they make no concealment, as we are very close to them,
> as are the Cyclopes and the savage tribes of the Giants.

> VII. 199–206

We have already been told of the gods' special love for the Phaeaceans, and how the people of Scheria themselves are nearly divine. Now we learn that the gods manifest that love by appearing to them not disguised, but in their pure forms. This gives us an indication of just how strongly Athene loves Odysseus, for she often converses with him in her pure, undisguised form. But it is not until Odysseus once again reaches Ithaca that she will be able to do so without fear of Poseidon's wrath.

Study Questions

1. Whom does Odysseus meet on his way to Alcinoös' palace?

2. How does Odysseus make his way to the palace without being noticed?

3. What advice does Athene give Odysseus concerning his supplication?

4. Why does Odysseus pause outside the palace?

5. What is the Phaeaceans' reaction to Odysseus' sudden appearance?

6. What does Odysseus do immediately after beseeching Arete?

7. What tale does Odysseus narrate briefly for the Phaeaceans?

8. Why does he tell this story?

9. What does Alcinoös propose concerning Nausikaa?

10. What extraordinary ability do the Phaeacean ships possess?

Answers

1. Odysseus encounters Athene disguised as a young girl.

2. Athene drifts a magical mist about him.

3. Athene tells Odysseus he should fall before Arete.

4. He admires the palace's beauty.

5. The Phaeaceans are startled by the sudden appearance of Odysseus.

6. He sits in a heap of ashes.

7. He tells them of his journey from Calypso's isle to Scheria.

8. Odysseus wants to explain to the Phaeaceans about the clothing he wears.

9. Alcinoös proposes that Odysseus marry her.

10. They may travel to any destination in the world and return in a single day.

Suggested Essay Topic

Examine the many scenes of hospitality in the *Odyssey*. How are they similar? How do they differ? What is significant about these differences? What commentary does each episode offer concerning the responsibilities of guest and host, such as gift-giving, nourishment, etc. What is the relationship between this motif and the distasteful situation occurring in Odysseus' home during his absence?

Book VIII

New Characters:

Demodocus: *the blind bard who entertains Odysseus and the Phaeaceans*

Laodamas: *the son of Alcinoös and one of the greatest athletes of Scheria*

Euryalus: *a Phaeacean athlete who insults Odysseus*

Summary

The next morning, Alcinoös orders a grand feast to be held in Odysseus' honor. Disguised as Alcinoös' herald, Pontonoös, Athene summons the mighty men of Scheria, including the twelve kings who reside on the island, to come to the feast. Alcinoös orders that a ship and companions be readied to speed Odysseus on his way. After his orders have been fulfilled, the Phaeacean king continues to entertain Odysseus.

The feast continues, and the assembled guests are entertained by the blind bard, Demodocus, renowned throughout Scheria as a singer gifted by the Muses. Demodocus sings of a quarrel which had broken out late in the war between Odysseus and Achilles. When hearing the song, Odysseus weeps secretly, detected by no one but Alcinoös.

Alcinoös then leads Odysseus and the Phaeaceans outside so that his guest can witness the athletic prowess of the youth of Scheria. After several contests have been performed, Laodamas, Alcinoös' son, suggests that Odysseus take part in the games.

Odysseus politely declines, but another athlete, Euryalus, insults Odysseus for declining. He suggests that Odysseus has led a life concerned solely with avarice and gain on the high seas, and that the attributes of manliness and sportsmanship are lacking in Odysseus. Sorely angered, Odysseus takes up a discus and hurls it much further than any other athlete had done in that day's competition. Provoked to fiery bitterness, Odysseus then rebukes Euryalus and challenges every athlete present to meet him in any competition whatsoever.

Alcinoös wisely steps forward and cools Odysseus, apologizing for Euryalus and offering Odysseus gifts from all the Phaeacean lords to console him in his homesick sorrow. He then commands Laodamas and the other Phaeacean dancers to perform for Odysseus.

While the Phaeaceans dance, Demodocus accompanies them by singing a tale of the gods. Helius, god of the sun, had informed Hephaestus, the lame god of blacksmiths, of his wife Aphrodite's unfaithfulness. It seems that the war god, Ares, had been making love to the goddess behind her husband's back. Infuriated, Hephaestus retired to his smithy and created a durable net that was so thin that it was invisible. He then fixed the trap around his bed so that it would constrict anyone who would lie there. While Hephaestus pretended to travel to the isle of Lemnos, Ares and Aphrodite met swiftly in Hephaestus' bed; soon they were trussed up in the master smith's indestructible coils. Meanwhile, Hephaestus himself, informed by Helius, returned to his palace and witnessed the adulterous pair ensnared in his trap. The angry blacksmith then called upon all the gods to witness the iniquitous affair so that he might regain the wedding presents he bestowed on Zeus for Aphrodite's hand; the goddesses, embarrassed by the situation, remained at home. When the gods arrived, they amused themselves greatly to the expense of the captive pair. Apollo asked Hermes if he would lie thus with Aphrodite with such consequences, and Hermes responded that no degree of exposure or punishment would keep him away from Aphrodite's embraces, if such opportunity presented itself. Poseidon, however, was not amused, and acted as a guarantee for Ares' responsibility to pay Hephaestus an adulterer's penalty. Hephaestus agreed to Poseidon's offer, and the pair, humiliated, fled from Olympus.

   With the tale concluded, Laodamas and the others also conclude their dancing. Afterwards, Euryalus offers Odysseus an apology, and awards him a handsome sword, for which Odysseus thanks him. The Phaeaceans again enter Alcinoös' palace, and, after Odysseus has bathed, received his gifts, and said farewell to Nausikaa, they resume their feasting. Odysseus entreats Demodocus to tell the tale of the Trojan Horse, and the blind bard complies readily, relating the Greeks' exit from the false wooden idol and their subsequent battles inside the walls of Troy. Odysseus again weeps to hear these Trojan stories. The matter is noticed once more by Alcinoös, who informs the Phaeaceans of Odysseus' sorrow. Alcinoös next entreats Odysseus to reveal his identity to the Phaeaceans and explain why the Trojan War brings him such sad remembrance. Alcinoös wonders whether it is because a relative or a dear friend of Odysseus has perished there.

Analysis

   Demodocus, although apparently a peripheral character, is a very significant figure in the *Odyssey*. First of all, we notice his relationship to Homer, who is depicted as a blind bard in the Homeric tradition. We learn much about the status of this profession through the Phaeaceans' treatment and high regard for the bard's art.

   Demodocus' storytelling introduces another motif that also runs fairly regularly throughout the *Iliad*: the contrast between mortal pathos and immortal buffoonery. In the *Iliad*, when the Greek and Trojan forces clash with graphic violence and bloodshed on the plains of Ilium, the gods quarrel over personal niceties. When the immortals are delivered a mortal wound, they have merely to float home and take it easy for a while, while the mortals must worry about the forlorn destination of their hapless souls. Even when the gods finally engage each other in a great battle, the result is more humorous than dramatic, as scholars have noted.

   Critics have noticed a similar dichotomy in Demodocus' stories. He sings two heated tales of Troy, both of which concern serious subject matter. The second story about the Trojan Horse ends in the sack and destruction of Troy. Contrasted to these is the story of Hephaestus being cuckolded by Aphrodite and Ares. Every character drawn by Demodocus in this narrative is a caricature. There is no real drama, and the characters lack human motivations and concerns; they are living in a world of comedy, where the tragic is a thing beyond their ken. For mortals, conversely, the comic moment is a brief one needed to lighten the mood of an otherwise somber existence.

Study Questions

1. What entertainment do the Phaeaceans find at Alcinoös' feast?

2. What task is undertaken by Alcinoös' herald throughout Book VIII?

3. What is the first story told by Demodocus?

4. What is Odysseus' reaction to Demodocus' tales of Troy?

5. Why is Odysseus annoyed while at the athletic field?

6. What action is taken by Odysseus to disprove Euryalus' accusatory insults?

7. How does Hephaestus learn about his wife's lewd conduct?

8. How does he confirm his suspicions?

9. Which of Demodocus' characters sympathizes most with the adulterous gods' imprisonment?

10. At the end of Book VIII, what does Alcinoös demand of Odysseus?

Answers

1. The Phaeaceans are entertained by Demodocus' singing.

2. He cares for Demodocus' needs.

3. Demodocus tells of a quarrel between Odysseus and Achilles.

4. He weeps secretly.

5. Euryalus insults him.

6.   He throws a discus an amazing distance.

7.   Helius informs him of his wife's lewd conduct.

8.   He sets a trap in his bed.

9.   Poseidon is the most sympathetic.

10. Alcinoös demands of Odysseus that he reveal his identity to the assembled Phaeaceans.

Suggested Essay Topics

Examine the character of Demodocus in Book VIII. What information does Homer relate to us concerning his profession? How did professional bards survive? Note Penelope's attempt to silence Phemius in Book I. What is significant about Telemachus' defense of Phemius' behavior, and how does this defense relate to Demodocus later in the narrative?

Book IX

New Character:

Polyphemus: *a Cyclops who devours Odysseus' men*

Summary

Odysseus reveals his identity to the Phaeaceans, and then begins recounting his tales from the time of his departure from Troy. Sailing to the northwest along the coast of the Aegean Sea, Odysseus and his fleet of twelve ships raided the Ciconian people, taking much booty and plunder. However, despite Odysseus' entreaties for his men to take to sea, his men did not obey him. The coastal Ciconians summoned their inland brothers, who came and waged a fierce battle against Odysseus' men, a struggle which eventually turned against the raiding Greeks. Odysseus lost over seventy men before reaching his ships and taking off once more to sea.

While sailing around the southern tip of Greece on the way to Ithaca, which lies to the northwest, Odysseus' fleet met a terrible storm, which blew them off course for nine days. They reached the

land of the Lotus-Eaters, who offered three of Odysseus' men some of their lotus plant to eat. The men complied, but immediately refused to leave their new locale because of the lotus flowers' enchantment. Odysseus dragged his wailing men back to the ships, and they again moved out to sea.

They came next to the land of the lawless Cyclopes, who lived solitary existences in cavernous dwellings. Odysseus' twelve ships beached themselves on an island not far from the mainland of the Cyclopes. Odysseus took his personal vessel alone to explore, and left his companions' vessels behind to await his return. Sailing around the island, Odysseus found the cave of the mighty Polyphemus. He chose twelve companions from his ship to accompany him, and went ashore to explore the cave. Inside, they found the master of the cave away, although there were many sheep and goats locked up in pens inside the cave. A tall, fenced-in yard enclosed an area immediately outside the cave.

Odysseus' men advised him to steal the cheese and livestock, and then to escape as quickly as possible. Odysseus, however, was eager to receive a gift from this mighty host, and so they waited for the Cyclops' arrival. When the enormous Polyphemus did arrive home from pasturing his flock, Odysseus and his men fled from the awesome sight of him. The Cyclops then rolled an enormous boulder across the entrance to his cave, one so heavy that all of Odysseus' men together could never budge it. After milking his goats and sheep, Polyphemus greeted his guests. Odysseus boldly requested a present from this hulk, demanding the rights due to strangers by Zeus's decree.

Scorning the gods, Polyphemus grasped two of Odysseus' men and slammed their heads against the ground. He then proceeded to eat them whole. When the brute had finished his feast and was in the midst of taking a nap, Odysseus planned to kill him, but reconsidered when he remembered the immovable boulder.

When the Cyclops awakened in the morning, he ate two more men before taking his sheep to pasture, leaving the dreaded boulder behind to block the exit. Odysseus hatched a plan, and went across the cave to where Polyphemus kept a felled olive tree. Odysseus and his men fashioned a long spike out of this, and hid it before the Cyclops returned home. When Polyphemus returned to his lair, he slew and devoured yet two more of Odysseus' men. After the monster had finished his grisly meal, Odysseus offered him a drink of wine from a silver mixing bowl. Odysseus had received this wine, which was unbelievably potent, from a Ciconian priest of Apollo whose life he had spared. One would normally dilute this wine in 95 percent water before drinking it. Now, Odysseus offered it unmixed to the mighty giant, who drank several draughts of it before collapsing in a drunken stupor. However, before he had finished his drinking, Polyphemus had asked Odysseus to tell him his name; the clever adventurer responded that his name was "Nobody."

With the Cyclops unconscious, Odysseus and four of his men grabbed the wooden spike and heated it in burning embers. They then thrust it firmly into the Cyclops' eye and blinded him. Awakening in agony, Polyphemus ripped the spike from his socket and screamed in agony to his fellow Cyclopes for aid. When they asked him if someone was antagonizing him, Polyphemus naturally replied that "Nobody" was doing so. Tricked into thinking that Polyphemus was calling to them for nothing more than a personal problem, the Cyclopes left their compatriot to his doom.

The enraged Cyclops then pushed the boulder away from the entrance and guarded the way with outstretched arms, hoping to catch Odysseus and his men as they fled with his sheep. Odysseus, however, attached his men to the bellies of the woolly sheep, one man beneath three sheep strapped together, and he attached himself to the belly of an enormous ram. In the morning, when the sheep and goats fled out of the cave to pasture, Polyphemus felt his animals' backs, but did not detect the men underneath them.

Odysseus and his men freed themselves from the sheep and herded the beasts down to the ship, where they quickly embarked and set out to sea. However, when they had pushed away from the island, Odysseus called out to taunt the Cyclops, who angrily hurled an enormous piece of rock at them. The boulder landed right off the bow, and the waves pushed the ship back to the shore. Odysseus quickly pushed off again, and when he had reached an even greater distance from the shore, the angry traveler again called to taunt Polyphemus, despite his crewmen's reproaches.

This time Odysseus told Polyphemus his true name and lands, and the Cyclops cursed him in his father Poseidon's name. It is in this way that Odysseus incurred the sea god's wrath, which prevented him from reaching his home for ten long years. After cursing Odysseus, Polyphemus hurled yet another rock at the ship. This boulder landed close to the stern, and pushed the ship away from Polyphemus toward the other part of the island where Odysseus' fleet awaited him. Greeting their companions eagerly, Odysseus' men divided up the spoils of the sheep. Odysseus was given the great ram he had ridden out of the cave, and he sacrificed it to Zeus on the beach. Soon afterwards, the ships set sail and left the Cyclopes' isle behind.

Analysis

In a narrative so preoccupied with hospitality and host-guest relations, we must view Polyphemus as the epitome of the poor host. His importance in the story rests significantly on this issue, and we see this most clearly when Odysseus first taunts the blinded Cyclops on his way out to sea:

> Cyclops, in the end it was no weak man's companions
> you were to eat by violence and force in your hollow
> cave, and your evil deeds were to catch up with you, and be

too strong for you, hard one, who dared to eat your own guests
in your own house, so Zeus and the rest of the gods have punished you.

IX. 475–79

This final rebuke is the moral of the Polyphemus story. We were given an indication of this very early in the tale, when, instead of heeding the thieving instincts of his companions, Odysseus relied on the responsibility expected of a host toward his guest. When Polyphemus entered the cave, Odysseus demanded his rights as a guest in the name of Zeus. Polyphemus, who believed the Cyclopes superior to the gods, had nothing to do with Zeus's mandates.

It is important to note that Odysseus stresses the lawless na-ture of the Cyclopes. The giant one-eyed creatures are chaotic bar-barians who have no system of government, but instead live in isolated seclusion. We cannot help but perceive the implied mes-sage of Odysseus: those who treat their guests poorly are creatures of chaos, and not ordered, civilized beings. Hospitality is a symbol of civilization; uncivil behavior toward one's guests is therefore a symbol of barbarism.

The secluded nature of the Cyclopes is also a commentary on Greek life from the epic poet himself. Homer, who stressed the importance of Greek unity so strongly in the *Iliad*, shows the dire fate awaiting a system of isolated city-states where each is a law unto itself. Polyphemus' neighbors fail to aid him in his distress, thinking his personal problems are of no concern of them. Just so, says Homer, will a lone polis cry for help, but when the other cities perceive that the victim's problems do not directly concern them, the surrounding states will ignore that call.

Study Questions

1. With how many ships does Odysseus depart from Troy?

2. Whom do they encounter first?

3. Whose land does Odysseus encounter after being blown off course for nine days?

4. What is the curse associated with that land?

5. What is the race and lineage of Polyphemus?

6. What outrage does he visit on his guests?

7. Why doesn't Odysseus kill Polyphemus?

8. What does he do to the Cyclops instead of killing him?

9. Why does Polyphemus stop the great ram on its way out of the cave?

10. What are the long-term consequences for Odysseus' treatment of Polyphemus?

Answers

1. Odysseus departs with 12 ships.

2. They first encounter the Ciconians.

3. He comes upon the land of the lotus-eaters.

4. Those who partake of the lotus forget their homeland.

5. He is a Cyclops and a son of Poseidon.

6. He eats the guests two at a time.

7. He knows that Polyphemus is the only one who can remove the door stop.

8. He drugs and blinds him.

9. Polyphemus wonders why the ram is the last one to depart instead of the first one, as he usually is.

10. Poseidon punishes him and keeps him from returning home for ten years.

Suggested Essay Topic

Book IX is the first section of a four-part narrative told by Odysseus himself to the Phaeaceans. What are the differences between Odysseus' narrative technique and that of the main narrator of the *Odyssey*? What are the similarities between the two? Does Odysseus' depiction of himself coincide with that of the main narrator? Explain the significance of your findings.

Book X

New Characters:

Aeolus: *the keeper of the magical bag of winds*

Antiphates: *king of the giant Laistrygones*

Eurylochus: *the leader of the expedition to Circe's dwelling*

Circe: *the sorcerous goddess of the isle Aeaea*

Elpenor: *a young crewman of Odysseus who dies after a drunken fall*

Summary

Aeolus, a king charged with caring for the world's winds, entertained Odysseus and his men for a month on his island. He lent Odysseus the magical bag that keeps the winds so that his fleet might move under the steady West Wind until it reached Ithaca. However, as the fleet was within sight of its home territory, Odysseus fell asleep, exhausted from manning the sails. His men,

jealous of their lord's success, thought that the bag of winds contained a secret gift given exclusively to Odysseus. They foolishly opened the bag, and released all of its winds at once. The fleet was blown all the way back to the Aeolian island. When Odysseus entreated Aeolus to help him once more, he was angrily turned away; Aeolus felt he had no right to help a wretch so hated by the gods.

Odysseus' fleet next journeyed to the land of the Laistrygones. The ships traveled down a narrow harbor surrounded by towering crags. Odysseus' own ship, however, was anchored away from the rest of the fleet. He sent three men forward as scouts, and these men encountered the daughter of Antiphates, king of the Laistrygones. She directed them to the great castle of her father, where they were amazed by the enormous size of the Laistrygones. Antiphates devoured one of the messengers, and called on his fellows to help him pursue the others. When the giants had reached the ships, they destroyed the fleet, carrying off every ship but Odysseus' own; the quick-thinking leader had cut cables and set off at once. His lone ship escaped intact.

The ship brought its mourning survivors to the island of Circe, Aeaea. There, Odysseus discovered a column of smoke drifting up from Circe's house, and sent out half his men, drawn by lot, to investigate. Eurylochus led the men to the stone house, where they heard a woman singing as she worked her loom. She invited the men inside her house; all complied but the suspicious Eurylochus. Circe drugged the men's wine and touched them with her wand, making them forget their home country and transforming them into pigs. She then proceeded to herd the swine, who retained their human minds, into her pig pen.

Eurylochus fled to Odysseus, who bravely traveled to Circe's abode alone in order to free his men. On his way there, he met the disguised Hermes, who lent him the moly plant, which would protect him from Circe's spells. Following Hermes' instructions, Odysseus entered the house and drank from Circe's drugged wine. Then, when she touched him with her wand, he drew his sword and made as if to attack her. She immediately begged for mercy, and, after swearing a great oath to inflict no further harm upon him, she led him to her bed. After they had made love, Circe attempted to feed Odysseus, but he would not partake of her meal until she freed his companions.

Circe agreed to do so, and the men, restored to human shape, wept to see Odysseus once more in their presence. Odysseus called the rest of his men from the ship, and the men eagerly obeyed, for they were glad to hear of their companions' rescue. Eurylochus remained pessimistic, but he returned to the house nonetheless.

Odysseus and his men remained with Circe for a year while recovering their strength. Afterwards, the men were very anxious about returning home. Odysseus begged his leave of Circe, who agreed to help him return to Ithaca. However, she warned him that he must first travel to the land of the dead in order to receive instructions from the Theban prophet, Teiresias, who retained his powers even after death. Odysseus wept to hear of the journey, and so did his men when they heard of it.

Before they headed towards their ship, a young crewman named Elpenor, disoriented from drink, awoke atop Circe's roof. He drunkenly fell off the side of the house, breaking his neck in the process. Leaving his corpse behind, Odysseus' men walked to their ship. There they met Circe, who had traveled faster than they had, bearing with her the sacrificial animals necessary for their communion with the dead.

Analysis

We are given another interesting twist on the host-guest relationship in Book X. Like Polyphemus, Circe abuses her guests severely. However, when Odysseus overcomes her, she becomes a perfect host. There is an interesting moment when Odysseus, though in the midst of receiving royal treatment from Circe and her maids, refuses to partake of his meal from her. This is because his men have not yet been restored to him, and still assume the shape of pigs. Only when this final reversal of fortunes in Odysseus' favor has been completed can he fully enjoy her hospitality.

Here the motif of hospitality and host-guest relations is used as a marker for a sign of trouble. For nowhere else in the *Odyssey* do we see a gracious host's meal spurned by a guest. This is a sign that Circe still stands on the threshold between antagonist and benefactor. As we can see, she becomes wholly benevolent to

Odysseus' party thereafter, caring for them wholeheartedly for a year's time. But the moment of final transition takes place during a rote scene of hospitality that is suddenly interrupted, a sign to the attentive reader or listener that something unexpected is about to take place.

Circe's role reversal from enemy to host inversely parallels an occurrence earlier in Book X. Aeolus, who was initially a benevolent and kind host to Odysseus and his men for a month's time, turns violently against the party when they return to his island. Although his reasons for changing his attitude are very different from those governing Circe's behavior, the episode as a whole negatively foreshadows the coming events on Circe's island.

Study Questions

1. Why does Aeolus rudely banish Odysseus from his island?

2. What calamity does Odysseus' fleet meet among the Laistrygones?

3. How does Odysseus learn of his crew's transformation by Circe?

4. How is he able to resist her magic?

5. Why does Odysseus refuse to partake of Circe's meal?

6. What is Eurylochus' reaction to Odysseus' news concerning his conquest of Circe?

7. How long does Odysseus remain on Aeaea?

8. What disturbing news does Circe break to Odysseus concerning his journey home?

9. What happens to Elpenor?

10. How do the men react to Odysseus' news concerning their journey?

Answers

1. He feels he has no right to assist one so hated by the gods.

2. All but one of his ships are destroyed.

3. Eurylochus escapes to inform him of the calamity.

4. Hermes lends him the moly plant.

5. He wants his men freed from their transformation first.

6. He angrily asserts that the men should flee Circe and ignore Odysseus' folly.

7. He remains on the island for one year.

8. He must first visit the realm of Hades.

9. He drunkenly falls off Circe's roof and breaks his neck.

10. They are heartbroken and sorrowful.

Suggested Essay Topic

The loyalty of Odysseus' crew is constantly in flux. Sometimes they follow him unswervingly, and other times they refuse to obey him and even conspire against him. Examine these critical moments throughout Odysseus' narrative. How significant are these moments in the plot's overall progression? What message are both Odysseus and Homer himself trying to drive home to their audiences by means of these many examples of loyalty and disloyalty?

Book XI

New Characters:

Teiresias: *prophet of Thebes who retained his prescience after death*

Anticleia: *Odysseus' mother*

Agamemnon: *commander of the Greek forces at Troy*

Achilles: *greatest hero of the Trojan War*

Ajax Telamonius: *burly hero of the Trojan War*

Summary

Odysseus departed from Aeaea and sailed to the ends of the earth in search of Hades' realm. Passing through the realm of the Cimmerians, which the sun never illuminates, Odysseus and his

men arrived on the outskirts of Hades' kingdom. They disembarked and prepared a drink offering for the dead spirits in a shallow pit. Following Circe's instructions perfectly, Odysseus attracted the spirits of the dead with the blood of sacrificed animals. While keeping the spirits away with his sword until Teiresias' arrival, Odysseus met the spirit of Elpenor. Elpenor explained that he was only a shadowy image of his former self, and begged Odysseus to bury him when his ship returned to Aeaea. Odysseus agreed to do so.

Teiresias appeared and warned Odysseus to keep his men away from the cattle of Helius on the isle of Thrinacea. If Odysseus failed to do so, his companions would perish, and he himself would return home in a stranger's ship after enduring much hardship. Teiresias also informed Odysseus of the future adventures he would undergo after he had returned home and established order in his household. Teiresias finally explained to Odysseus that he could converse with any spirits whom he allowed to drink of his blood offering.

After Teiresias departed into the shadows, Odysseus spoke with his mother, Anticleia. Anticleia told him of matters at home, and that she had died in her longing for him. When he had finished speaking with his mother, Odysseus began to interview the spirits of deceased queens whom Persephone, queen of the Underworld, sent to greet Odysseus. Among the queens he met was Tyro, the grandmother of Nestor, who lay secretly with Poseidon to conceive Nestor's father, Neleus. He also met Epikaste, the mother of Oedepodes, who slew his father and married his mother. (These became Jocasta and Oedipus in Sophocles' tragedy, *Oedipus Rex*.)

Odysseus also met Nestor's mother, Chloris, whose daughter Pero's hand was sought by the prophet, Melampous. Neleus had sent Melampous to steal Iphicles' cattle as a gift to win Pero, but Iphicles captured Melampous and forced him to prophesy for a full year before he released the augur.

Odysseus met Leda, mother of Castor and Polydeuces. He also saw Iphimedeia, whose enormous children Otus and Ephialtes threatened the gods themselves until they were slain by Apollo. Among others met by Odysseus was Ariadne, the doomed lover of Theseus.

In the midst of the catalog, Odysseus suddenly brings his tale to a halt. Tired, he entreats the Phaeaceans to allow him to sleep so that he might soon depart for Ithaca. Alcinoös and Arete, highly impressed by Odysseus' storytelling, tell him that the Phaeaceans will bestow even more treasure on their guest. Persuaded by the prospect of returning home with even further wealth, Odysseus agrees not to rush his homecoming. Alcinoös also induces Odysseus to continue his story.

Odysseus' tale resumes. After the queens' spirits departed, Odysseus was greeted by the spirit of Agamemnon himself. Agamemnon told Odysseus of his murder by Aegisthus and Clytemnestra; his wife had also personally slain the priestess Cassandra. Agamemnon then wished Odysseus luck on his own homecoming, envious that Penelope would be more faithful than Clytemnestra had been.

Odysseus next met Achilles and other deceased heroes from the Trojan conflict. Achilles asked for news of his family, and Odysseus informed the hero of his son Neoptolemus' bravery in battle. Achilles, satisfied with Odysseus' news, strode away with pride. Among the Greek heroes present in the crowd was Ajax Telamonius, who had slain himself after Thetis, Achilles' mother, had chosen Odysseus to receive her son's armor instead of the brawny hero. Still angry even after death at Odysseus' victory, Ajax refused to answer Odysseus' entreaties to speak with him.

Turning aside from Ajax, Odysseus witnessed other souls in the land of the dead. He saw the spirit of Minos, who had become the judge of the dead. He also perceived Tantalus, who was denied the water and fruit that were constantly within his reach. He saw the anguished spirit of Sisyphus, who rolled an enormous boulder up a hill, but, after it reached the summit, the rock rolled back to its point of origin. Odysseus also met a shadowy reflection of Heracles, despite the fact that the demigod's true soul resided on Olympus. Heracles recalled the time when he too had visited the Underworld while still alive; he had been forced to drag the dog Cerberus from the land of the dead.

Fearing that Persephone might punish him for lingering, Odysseus summoned his men to prepare their return to Aeaea. His ship sailed up the river which had carried them to the Underworld, and then they put out into the open sea.

Analysis

Book XI of the *Odyssey* set the precedent for the most imitated epic convention of later ages: the trip to the Underworld. Virgil would copy much from Homer when recounting Aeneas' trip to Elysium, and Dante would devote his entire *Inferno* to the motif.

But for Homer himself, the scenes featuring Odysseus down among the spirits of the dead serve another purpose. They allow the poet to compress story after story about new characters into the middle of his narrative. In the *Iliad*, we often received snatches of stories about characters foreign to the main narrative, such as Bellerophontes. However, when Odysseus relates his visit to the Underworld, Homer includes more separate tales in a shorter space than he ever had done before.

The entrance of Agamemnon, Achilles, and the other Greek heroes produces a strong link to the narrative action of the *Iliad*. We should not be surprised at this point to hear Agamemnon, when relating his murder, to compare Odysseus' family with his own; this theme runs fairly regularly throughout the *Odyssey*. We see once more the negative correlation between each family member of the Atreus house and his or her counterpart in Odysseus' family.

Agamemnon speaks to Odysseus:

> And yet you, Odysseus, will never be murdered by your wife.
> The daughter of Ikarios, circumspect Penelope,
> is all too virtuous and her mind is stored with good thoughts.
> Ah well. She was only a young wife when we left her
> and went off to the fighting, and she had an infant child then
> at her breast. That child now must sit with the men and be counted.
> Happy he! for his dear father will come back, and see him,
> and he will fold his father in his arms, as is right. My wife
> never even let me feed my eyes with the sight of
> my own son, but before that I myself was killed by her.
>
> XI. 444–53

Here we see the link between Penelope and Clytemnestra leads directly to the comparison of Telemachus and Orestes. Agamemnon merely perpetuates a model that was begun by the other characters of the *Odyssey* who were concerned with the commander's fate.

Perhaps the most heartfelt message that Homer gives us in these Underworld scenes comes during Odysseus' interview with Achilles. Odysseus admires Achilles' ability to command his fellow Greeks even after death, but Achilles sharply rebukes him:

> O shining Odysseus, never try to console me for dying.
> I would rather follow the plow as thrall to another
> man, one with no land allotted him and not much to live on,
> than be a king over all the perished dead.
>
> XI. 488–91

Here is Homer's utmost expression of life's inestimable value: the lowest plight of the living is greater than the most fortunate circumstances of the dead.

Study Questions

1. Whom does Odysseus first meet in the Underworld?

2. What advice does Teiresias offer Odysseus concerning his future stay on Thrinacea?

3. Why didn't Anticlea initially recognize Odysseus?

4. How did Anticlea die?

5. Why did the souls of the deceased queens appear to Odysseus?

6. Whose death does Agamemnon add to the list of Clytemnestra's crimes?

7. What comforting news does Odysseus relate to Achilles?

8. Why doesn't Ajax Telamonius approach Odysseus?

9. What is the curse of Tantalus?

10. Of what does Odysseus' presence in Hades' realm remind Heracles?

Answers

1. The first person he meets is Elpenor.

2. He must not slaughter the livestock of Helius.

3. She had not partaken yet of his blood offering.

4. Anticlea died of longing for her son.

5. Persephone, queen of the dead, sent them to him.

6. Agamemnon adds to the list of Clytemnestra's crimes the death of Cassandra, the prophetess of Apollo.

7. Odysseus tells Achilles about the heroism of Neoptolemus.

8. He is still bitter at Odysseus for winning the armor of Achilles.

9. He is unable to drink the water he is immersed in or eat the fruit growing within his reach.

10. It reminds Heracles of his own journey to Hades' realm while he was still alive.

Suggested Essay Topic

Throughout the *Odyssey*, Odysseus' curiosity is one of his most endearing traits. Note the conflict between fear and curiosity that he experiences throughout Book XI. What do we learn about his character here? Does his curiosity ever seem obsessive? When do we see his curiosity in a negative light, and when do we see it in a positive light?

Book XII

New Characters:

Scylla: *a horrendous monster with six heads extended on elongated necks*

Charybdis: *a terrible creature that takes the form of a devouring whirlpool*

Helius: *god of the sun*

Summary

Odysseus' men, having left the Underworld, arrived once more on Circe's isle, Aeaea. There they immediately set about retrieving and burning Elpenor's body, as his spirit had requested. Circe met Odysseus and crew down by their ship, and pulled Odysseus aside to advise him on his upcoming journey home.

She warned him of the Sirens, whose singing lured men to their island, where they would listen to the women's voices until they died. She instructed him to stop his men's ears with wax, but, if he wanted to hear their voices himself, he could do so if his men first tied him tightly to the mast pole. She warned him next of the dreaded crossing of Scylla and Charybdis. Odysseus' ship would cross between two mighty crags that were swept by a raging current. If they steered one way, they would be sucked into Charybdis' whirlpool. If they steered the other way, they would lose six men to the ravenous appetite of Scylla, whose six heads would reach down on long necks to snatch men from the ship. Odysseus asked if there were some way to battle Scylla, but Circe advised him to push onward rather than fight this immortal creature. Finally, Circe warned Odysseus to avoid the cattle of Helius on Thrinacea, just as Teiresias had previously warned him. If they slaughtered the sun god's cattle, Odysseus' companions would be destroyed.

Odysseus' men set out finally from Aeaea, pushed on by a strong wind sent from Circe. As they approached the Sirens' isle, Odysseus warned his men of the danger and stopped their ears with wax. He himself listened to their enchanted music while tied to the mast, and his men tied him even tighter when he begged to join the women who sang so sweetly and enticed him with the promise of infinite knowledge.

After Odysseus' ship left the peril of the Sirens behind, it approached the perilous sea crags inhabited by Scylla and Charybdis. Odysseus strengthened his men's resolve to travel through the dreaded pass, and warned them to avoid Charybdis. However, he failed to inform them of Scylla, for he was afraid they would lose control of the ship in their fear. Despite Circe's warning, Odysseus donned his armor and weapons to stave off the coming doom. But when the ship passed under Scylla's lair, the sea beast snatched six men too quickly for Odysseus to act. They screamed helplessly to him as the ship continued its course through the treacherous pass.

The ship sailed clear of the dangerous waters, but came within sight of Thrinacea. Odysseus begged his men to avoid the island, but Eurylochus demanded they be allowed to rest and eat on the shores of the island. Odysseus gave in, but demanded they swear never to touch Helius' cattle and sheep.

However, a terrible storm began that evening, and strong winds continued to blow for a month, detaining Odysseus and his men on the island. Odysseus' men ran out of food and resorted to hunting fish and birds. One day, Odysseus set off on a retreat to pray to the gods for aid. The gods answered by drifting him off to sleep. While he was away, Eurylochus induced the men to stave off starvation by killing the cattle. By the time Odysseus awakened, the men had already sacrificed the cattle, much to their leader's anguish.

Helius' daughters, who herded the god's flocks, informed their father of the outrage done to his creatures. Helius, in turn, demanded that Zeus punish the perpetrators; if the men were not punished, Helius would turn his rays away from the world and into Hades' realm. Zeus, fearing his threat, agreed to chastise the wrongdoers.

When the winds died down, Odysseus' ship left Thrinacea. After they were far out to sea, Zeus summoned a storm and blasted Odysseus' ship, killing all of his companions. Odysseus himself drifted away on a makeshift raft comprising the ship's mast and keel. He floated all the way back to Charybdis, where his raft was sucked into the whirlpool. Odysseus hung desperately to the overhanging branch of a fig tree on the crag adjacent to Charybdis. He held on for hours until Charybdis regurgitated his raft. Odysseus released his hold on the branch, and paddled his raft out of the

deadly pass. He drifted for nine days until, on the tenth, he became stranded on Calypso's isle, Ogygia. It is here that Odysseus'
tale to the Phaeaceans comes to an end.

Analysis

Odysseus' perseverance and fortitude are exemplified in the
scene before Scylla and Charybdis in Book XII. Odysseus' duty as
captain of the ship supersedes his personal relationship with his
men; he must therefore keep them ignorant of Scylla's presence
until it is too late. Yet Homer shows us the anguish he experiences
concerning this decision, which was not made callously or indif-
ferently. Odysseus dons his armor and equipment despite Circe's
assertion of Scylla's invulnerability. This is because Odysseus refuses to surrender, no matter the opposition facing him. He will
dare anything, even the impossible, to try and save his crew.

When the terrible moment comes, and Scylla surprises
Odysseus by attacking behind him rather than near the ship's prow
where he was stationed, we can feel the terrible pangs of regret in
Odysseus' spirit, even still as he retells the tale to the Phaeaceans.
Even after the event, perhaps, his men knew nothing of Odysseus'
forewarning by Circe. But his personal guilt consumes him, and
this is evident not from a direct, stated reflection on Odysseus' part,
but from the very description he provides of the horrid scene:

> We in fear of destruction kept our eyes on Charybdis,
> but meanwhile Skylla out of the hollow vessel snatched six
> of my companions, the best of them for strength and hands' work,
> and when I turned to look at the ship, with my other companions,
> I saw their feet and hands from below, already lifted
> high above me, and they cried out to me and called me
> by name, the last time they ever did it, in heart's sorrow.
>
>   * * *
>
> . . . Right in her doorway she ate them up. They were screaming
> and reaching out their hands to me in this horrid encounter.
> That was the most pitiful scene that these eyes have looked on
> in my sufferings as I explored the routes over the water.
>
>   XII. 244–59

The image that burned itself into Odysseus' mind was primarily that of his men's supplications to him, their cry of distress. This call must have made Odysseus feel a bitter sense of betrayal towards his followers, who relied on him to see them through all danger. Yet they remained ignorant of a peril known only to their silent master. What makes the image the "most pitiful scene" Odysseus has witnessed on his adventures is not merely the physical slaughter, which he saw much more intimately in Polyphemus' cave. It is rather the terrible burden of guilt that assailed him at the moment of his companions' death.

Study Questions

1. What aid does Circe lend Odysseus before he departs from Aeaea?

2. How do Odysseus' men become immune to the Sirens' singing?

3. Why is Odysseus tied to the mast?

4. What choice must Odysseus make when passing though the perilous sea cliffs?

5. What decision does he make?

6. In what way does Odysseus ignore Circe's advice concerning Scylla?

7. Why does Odysseus stop on Thrinacea, despite the many warnings he has been given?

8. Where is he when his men devour the cattle of Helius?

9. In what way does Helius coerce Zeus to punish Odysseus' men?

10. Why does Odysseus end his story with his arrival on Calypso's isle?

Answers

1. She gives him advice concerning the Sirens, Scylla and Charybdis, and the isle Thrinacea.

2. Odysseus plugs their ears with beeswax.

3. Odysseus is tied to the mast so that he may safely listen to the Sirens' singing.

4. He must choose to encounter either Scylla or Charybdis.

5. He chooses to face Scylla.

6. He prepares to battle the monster.

7. Eurylochus demands the crew be permitted to rest and eat on shore.

8. He is away on a retreat imploring the aid of the gods.

9. Helius threatens to transfer his light to the Underworld.

10. He had previously told Alcinoös and Arete the rest of the story from Calypso's isle to the present.

Suggested Essay Topic

Examine Odysseus' relationship to the supernatural universe surrounding him. At what moments does he lack control over his surroundings? At what moments does he seem in command of his own fate and that of his companions? What message may we infer from Homer's treatment of Odysseus' relationship with the gods? What do we learn about the poet's views on human nature and its interaction with forces beyond its control?

Book XIII

Summary

Odysseus ends his tale, and the Phaeaceans, highly impressed, return to their homes for the evening. The next morning, at Alcinoös' behest, the Phaeacean lords return to the palace to render Odysseus even costlier gifts than they had before. These are loaded aboard the ship reserved for Odysseus' journey home. Alcinoös then begins another feast in Odysseus' honor.

Odysseus, impatient to be on his way home, waits anxiously for evening to arrive. As Alcinoös yet again toasts Odysseus on his journey, the adventurer does not even stop to drink; he hands Arete his cup, says a quick farewell, and strides out of the hall and down

to the ship. The Phaeaceans set blankets for him on the ship's deck, and the weary Odysseus falls into a deep, oblivious sleep. The Phaeaceans row their powerful ship all night long and miraculously arrive in an enclosed, Ithacan bay before sunrise. They gently disembark the sleeping Odysseus and his many Phaeacean gifts; the crewmen then sail quickly away from Ithaca.

Poseidon, enraged over Odysseus' rescue, approaches Zeus. Although the sea god realizes that Zeus had ordained Odysseus' eventual homecoming, Poseidon wishes to punish the Phaeaceans for their involvement in the matter. He asks Zeus if he might be allowed to petrify the returning Phaeacean ship and then pile a mountain over the top of Alcinoös' city. This would indeed coincide with a prophecy told to Alcinoös concerning a possible fate for the Phaeaceans. While Zeus agrees that Poseidon should punish the Phaeaceans, he does not believe he should go so far as to drop a mountain on them. Poseidon travels to Scheria and turns the ship returning from Ithaca to stone before the Phaeacean people's very eyes. Alcinoös, recognizing the portent, discourages the Phaeaceans from ever transporting strangers again. He also commands them to sacrifice to Poseidon, in the hope that he might relent from fulfilling the second half of the prophecy: namely, covering the city with a mountain.

Meanwhile, Odysseus awakens on Ithaca, but Athene drifts a mist over him that makes the land seem unfamiliar to him. Odysseus, despairing over his fortune, curses the Phaeaceans for abandoning him on an unknown shore. When Athene approaches him disguised as a young boy, Odysseus eagerly asks the seeming lad what land he has entered. After cataloging the nature of the place, Athene finally admits that he is on Ithaca.

Odysseus, though inwardly rejoicing, decides to pretend he is an unfortunate traveler who was abandoned by Phoenician escorts on this island of which he is only remotely familiar. After enjoying his performance, Athene appears to Odysseus in her pure form, remarking on his propensity to assume disguises. Odysseus, glad to be rejoined by his divine companion, asks her why she had abandoned him to his dismal fate since the time of Troy's fall. She explains to him how she has indeed been helping him, but that her work was performed secretly so as not to arouse the powerful Poseidon's attention.

Athene then helps Odysseus hide his many treasures in a cave located in the enclosed harbor where the Phaeaceans deposited Odysseus. She next informs him of the situation in his home and also tells him about Telemachus' journey to Sparta. Athene advises Odysseus to keep his presence in Ithaca a secret until he comes upon a way to destroy the suitors. Odysseus agrees to her strategy.

Athene transforms his outer appearance into that of an old beggar so that Odysseus might travel through Ithaca in complete disguise. She then commands Odysseus to go to the dwelling of Eumaeus the loyal swineherd. Athene herself departs for Sparta so that she might convince Telemachus to return to his home.

Analysis

Odysseus' arrival on Ithaca is the midpoint of the *Odyssey*. As such, it is only appropriate that symbolic foreshadowing run through the scene between Odysseus and Athene. We have seen thus far Odysseus' wanderings from Troy to Ithaca. Now we must prepare ourselves for Odysseus' adventures in Ithaca itself.

Deception and illusion will feature prominently in the remaining books. Therefore, when Odysseus finally returns home, it is appropriate that he does not wake up joyful in the knowledge of his homecoming. Rather, he is immediately deceived by Athene's disorienting mist and falls into despair. Once Odysseus knows the truth about his arrival on Ithaca, he himself decides to engage in deception; this goes on until Athene dispels all illusions through her divine self-revelation.

This mirrors the events of Books XIII-XXIV in miniature. Odysseus does not receive the glorious, heroic homecoming that he had longed for during his wanderings. Instead, he must endure further suffering and hardship. He will overcome his opposition through disguise and deception until Athene dispels all illusions and all conflict by the end of the poem.

Of course, we must realize that Odysseus himself, however much he had longed for a peaceful homecoming, would not have been satisfied with simply waltzing into his palace and announcing his homecoming; as Athene points out, Odysseus would have employed deception to probe the thoughts of his family and subjects whether or not the suitors had plagued his household. This is manifested in his immediate recourse to deception upon learning of his long-awaited arrival on Ithaca. He concocts a complicated tale about his life to tell the young boy / Athene; the tale, oddly enough, resembles his actual life and circumstances in a few places. Athene, reverting immediately to her true form, remarks on

Odysseus' strange behavior in terms of endearment. Stroking his head as a mother would her son, she says:

> It would be a sharp one, and a stealthy one, who would ever get past you
> in any contriving; even if it were a god against you.
> You wretch, so devious, never weary of tricks, then you would not
> even in your own country give over your ways of deceiving
> and your thievish tales. They are near to you in your very nature.
> XIII. 291–95

This is certainly not a rebuke on Athene's part. Such a criticism would be hypocrisy coming from a goddess whose art of deception is matched only by Odysseus' own. The two of them, god and mortal, share a unique relationship, and we can see in this scene how deeply each cares for the other in a way that is more kindred than religious.

Athene informs Odysseus that it is "in your very nature" to employ guile and deception. That single remark will be displayed countless times in the narrative to come as Odysseus invents one tale after another when interviewing his family and servants. Therefore, it is only appropriate that a scene of illusion and mutual deception pervade Odysseus' wakening moments on Ithaca. These qualities are not merely tools employed by the wandering adventurer; they are his very being.

Study Questions

1. What does Alcinoös suggest to the Phaeaceans after Odysseus ends his tale?

2. What is Odysseus' mood during the next day of feasting?

3. What does Odysseus do while aboard the Phaeacean vessel?

4. In what strange way do the Phaeacean seamen drop Odysseus off at Ithaca?

5. Why is he unable to recognize his surroundings when he first perceives Ithaca?

6. What nervous activity does Odysseus perform concerning his treasure?

7. In what guise does Athene appear to Odysseus?

8. What important news does she deliver to him while she is in that guise?

9. What is Odysseus' first action after learning of his arrival on Ithaca?

10. What does Athene do to Odysseus at the end of Book XIII?

Answers

1. He suggests that they endow Odysseus with even more gifts.

2. He is anxious and impatient to begin his journey.

3. He sleeps.

4. They disembark Odysseus and his goods without waking him.

5. Athene alters his perception so as to make the island unfamiliar to him.

6. He counts it to make sure the Phaeaceans have taken none of it away with them.

7. Athene appears as a young shepherd boy.

8. She tells him he is on Ithaca.

9. He assumes a disguise.

10. She transforms him into an old beggar.

Suggested Essay Topic

Analyze the scenes where Odysseus employs deception in Books IX-XIII. What do we learn about Odysseus' character through his use of deception, disguise, and false storytelling?

Book XIV

New Character:

Eumaeus: *Odysseus' loyal swineherd*

Summary

Odysseus sets out for the shelter of Eumaeus the swineherd as per Athene's instructions. The faithful and loyal swineherd has kept Odysseus' pigs in order and has tended them skillfully. As Odysseus approaches the crude dwelling, he is accosted by Eumaeus' dogs; the swineherd himself, however, quickly comes to his rescue and brings him to his dwelling.

Eumaeus cares for Odysseus' needs, feeding him immediately upon bringing him into his house. As he speaks to the disguised Odysseus, Eumaeus constantly makes references to his beloved master, whom he asserts is lost and roaming the world in misery. When Odysseus requests Eumaeus' master's name, the swineherd reveals Odysseus' own name. Yet the swineherd bitterly warns his guest not to suggest that he has heard of Odysseus' imminent re-

turn. Eumaeus and other loyal followers of Odysseus have had enough of being constantly duped by lying beggars.

In spite of Eumaeus' warning, Odysseus embarks on a false tale about how he himself had heard of Odysseus in his travels. Odysseus tells Eumaeus that he is the son of a wealthy Cretan named Castor. Despite his illegitimate birth, the storyteller continues, he had risen to power in Crete and accompanied the prince Idomeneus to the Trojan War. After fighting at Troy for ten years, the narrator stopped only briefly at Crete, and then journeyed to Egypt and sailed down the Nile. There he met disaster, for his men pillaged outlying fields despite the narrator's warning, and the Egyptians swiftly punished them the following day. However, the narrator found favor with the Egyptian king and prospered in his house for seven years. From there, the narrator accompanied a crafty Phoenician to his home in Asia Minor. After spending a year with his new host, the narrator set out with the Phoenician to Libya, where the Phoenician secretly planned to sell the narrator into slavery. However, Zeus sent a storm that destroyed the Phoenician vessel, and the narrator was cast adrift on the seas. After floating on a makeshift raft for nine days, the narrator landed on the shores of Thesprotia, a mainland region in southwestern Epirus not far to the northeast of Ithaca. There, the narrator befriended the Thesprotian king, Pheidon, who told the narrator that he was preparing a splendid homecoming for Odysseus, who was taking a brief retreat at a nearby city. However, before Odysseus returned to the city, the narrator joined a group of sailors heading past Ithaca for the isle of Doulichion. These bad men also planned to sell the narrator into slavery and tied him up while they took an evening meal on the shores of Ithaca. The narrator escaped their clutches and wandered through Ithaca until he arrived at the swineherd's dwelling.

Eumaeus, while sympathizing with Odysseus' tale, does not believe the part about Odysseus' presence in Thesprotia and discourages his guest from speaking such lies in the future. Nevertheless, he continues to care for him, and when the other swineherds return from their daily rounds, Eumaeus prepares a great feast for them all in his guest's honor. After all have eaten well, they bed down for the evening. A cold storm arises, and Odysseus tests Eumaeus to see whether he will offer his guest a warm mantle. He tells a story of how Menelaus, Odysseus, and other Greeks including himself had been stationed one evening in the marshy field surrounding Troy. The narrator had asked Odysseus for some way to procure a mantle for himself. Odysseus had cleverly sent one of the other Greek spies on an errand to the Greek camp, and the narrator was able to seize the discarded bedding of the messenger.

Acting upon the hint, Eumaeus does indeed bestow an extra mantle on his guest, but then the swineherd himself goes outside into the cold night to personally oversee the welfare of the pigs. He lays down and sleeps among the droves of swine.

Analysis

Odysseus' false storytelling is a key feature of Book XIV, just as it had been in the preceding book. Once again, we see Odysseus inventing tales about his past life that often incorporate key instances from his actual life and experiences. For example, the narrator of his false tale had also been a fighter at Troy. His false persona also had problems controlling the selfish impulses of his crewmen. Just as Odysseus himself had troubles commanding his men to flee with their prizes from the conquered Ciconians (Book IX), so too is his persona unable to command his raiding forces on the Aegyptus (Nile) River (XIV. 259–65). In both instances, the raiding parties encounter swift reprisal from their former victims on the following day. Odysseus lost over seventy men in the disaster; his persona lost his entire company.

An even more remarkable similarity occurs when Odysseus describes the destruction of the Phoenician ship en route to Libya. Here, Odysseus depicts the destruction wrought by Zeus' storm with the exact words he used in Book XII to describe his own shipwreck at sea:

> Zeus with thunder and lightning together crashed on our vessel,
> and, struck by the thunderbolt of Zeus, she spun in a circle,
> and all was full of brimstone. The men were thrown in the water,
> and bobbing like sea crows they were washed away on the running

waves all around the black ship, and the god took away their
homecoming.

XIV. 305–309

This is an exact quote from XII. 415–19. One might argue that this
is simply a reflection of the formulae employed by Homeric bards
to describe a shipwreck, and not any conscious derivation from
life experience on the part of Odysseus' character. However, the
insertion of material from Odysseus' past narrative to the
Phaeaceans into his present narrative to Eumaeus continues from
there. Just as Odysseus had been swept away on a mast for nine
days until reaching his destination on Calypso's isle, so too does
his persona undergo an identical experience before landing on
Thesprotia. This depiction does not mimic the Book XII version
exactly, so we can see that Odysseus is consciously integrating seg-
ments either in whole or in part from one narrative to the other
and enhancing them to fit his fabricated narrative.

In this way, we see that Odysseus' "lies" are never wholly false,
but always include some aspect of the truth. Just as a disguised
Odysseus is still a true Odysseus covered with fictional enhance-
ments, so too are Odysseus' storytelling personae aspects of his
true personality that have been modified through the inclusion of
fictional elements.

Study Questions

1. What happens to Odysseus as he approaches the swineherd's
    dwelling?

2. What actions on the part of the suitors affect Eumaeus per-
    sonally?

3. What warning does Eumaeus give the disguised Odysseus
    before revealing his master's name to his guest?

4. What events have prompted Eumaeus to make this warn-
    ing?

5. What island does Odysseus' narrator claim as his home?

6. In what country did his narrator first meet disaster after the
    Trojan War?

7. Where did his narrator hear of Odysseus during his wanderings?

8. Why does Odysseus tell his false story about the Greeks at Troy?

9. How does Eumaeus react to the story?

10. Why does Eumaeus leave his dwelling during the stormy night?

Answers

1. Odysseus is assaulted by Eumaeus' dogs.

2. They consume the best of his swine.

3. Eumaeus advises Odysseus not to suggest that he knows of his master's whereabouts.

4. Many travelers have lied concerning Odysseus' fate.

5. Odysseus' narrator claims Crete as his home.

6. The narrator met disaster in Egypt.

7. He heard of Odysseus in Thesprotia.

8. Odysseus wishes to test Eumaeus to see if he will lend him a mantle.

9. He lends Odysseus a spare mantle.

10. He wishes to personally oversee the welfare of the pigs by sleeping outside with them.

Suggested Essay Topic

Examine Odysseus' second story about the mantle. What is significant about his depictions of both himself (the real Odysseus) and his persona in the narrative? Where do the ironies lie when we consider the fact that Odysseus himself is telling this false story? What insights do we gain about Odysseus through his telling of this story?

Book XV

New Characters:

Theoclymenus: *a fugitive prophet from Argos*

Peraeus: *a loyal friend of Telemachus*

Summary

Athene travels to Sparta and visits Telemachus in a dream. She tells him to take his leave of Menelaus quickly and return home so that he need not fear for the welfare of his goods. She informs him that Eurymachus has given the most presents to Icarius, Penelope's father; Telemachus had best return home in case Penelope decides to give some of her son's wealth to her prospective husband.

Telemachus awakens, and in the morning he and Peisistratus take their leave of Menelaus and Helen. However, the Spartan king first bestows a golden goblet and silver bowl forged by Hephaestus to Telemachus as guest gifts. Helen gives him a lovely gown which could be worn by Telemachus' future wife. As Telemachus and Peisistratus mount their chariot, an eagle bearing a captive goose flies by them on their right side. Helen interprets this as a sign of Odysseus' imminent return and the fulfillment of his vengeance against the suitors.

Telemachus rides for two days back to Pylus, where he asks Peisistratus to drop him off at his ship so that he might board it quickly and avoid a laborious leave-taking from Nestor. Although Peisistratus knows his father will be angry, he assists his new friend by leaving him by his ship. After Peisistratus has departed for his father's house, Telemachus' men prepare the ship for its voyage. While Telemachus is pouring a libation to the gods, he is visited by Theoclymenus, a prophet in a long line of prophets who is presently a fugitive from the region of Argos. The prophet's ancestor, Melampous, had sought and won the hand of Nestor's sister years ago; Melampous then migrated to Argos. Theoclymenus himself has slain a man who has many kinsmen. Fleeing their wrath, Theoclymenus requests passage on Telemachus' ship. The young son of Odysseus grants the fugitive's wish to accompany him to Ithaca. Telemachus' ship then sets out and heads for Ithaca. It sails on into the night in the hope of avoiding the suitors' ambush; Athene had previously warned Telemachus of this imminent danger.

Meanwhile, Odysseus again tests Eumaeus. Odysseus suggests that he should leave the swineherds' dwelling and head for the main city, where he can beg from the suitors. Eumaeus quickly dissuades him of this idea and keeps him sheltered in his midst.

Odysseus and Eumaeus stay up all night telling stories. Eumaeus tells Odysseus the story of his life. He was a prince of the island of Syria, whose homeland was visited by Phoenician traders. One of the traders made a pact with a Phoenician slave in Eumaeus' household; he agreed to free the bondswoman and restore her to her homeland. In recompense, the slave would steal treasure to give the traders; she also agreed to turn over her charge, Eumaeus himself, to be sold as a slave wherever the Phoenician men desired.

After the Phoenicians had finished a year of trading, they prepared to depart from Syria. The slave woman stole golden vessels from the palace and led the young Eumaeus out of the palace and down to the Phoenician ship. The ship sailed away from Syria, but the slave woman died on board without reaching her homeland; her body was cast into the sea. Eumaeus himself was sold to Laertes in Ithaca, where he was greatly cared for by Anticleia, who treated him almost as well as she did her own children.

When Odysseus and Eumaeus have finished their talking, they sleep for the few remaining hours until dawn. Meanwhile, Telemachus arrives on Ithaca, having successfully avoided the suitors' ambush. At Athene's behest, he asks his companions to continue around the coast of Ithaca to the city, where the ship might be returned to its owner. Telemachus himself must set out on foot for Eumaeus' dwelling, as per Athene's instructions. Before the men have departed, Telemachus witnesses another portent: a falcon flies by on Telemachus' right side bearing a captured pigeon in its talons. Theoclymenus interprets the portent as a sign of Telemachus' family's continued dominance in Ithaca. Pleased with the reading, Telemachus commands Peraeus, one of his loyal comrades, to care for Theoclymenus in the city until Telemachus fetches him later.

After this, Telemachus' companions embark and sail with

Theoclymenus to the city. Telemachus himself journeys on foot to the dwelling of Eumaeus, where the loyal swineherd sleeps faithfully with his master's pigs.

Analysis

We receive another amusing twist on the theme of hospitality in Book XV, one which we caught a glimpse of in Book XIII and which we see even more fully now. Polyphemus and Circe (Books IX and X) were symbols of malevolent hosts, a serious crime in Homer's world. Menelaus and Nestor represent the other end of the spectrum: the overly benevolent host. It is all Telemachus can do to wrench himself away from Menelaus, and when he approaches Pylus, he asks Peisistratus to help him to avoid Nestor "for fear the old man in his affection will keep me / in his house longer than I wish. But I must make my way quickly" (XV. 200–201). After having been detained in Sparta for longer than he would have liked, Telemachus knows the verbose Nestor will make no end of his farewells.

We are certainly intended to smile at these scenes, as we were in Book XIII when Odysseus impatiently waited for yet another Phaeacean feast to end so that he might make his way home at last. The epic simile used to describe Odysseus' anticipation was that of a man who has labored long in his field until he is released from his toil by the sunset. So too, suggests Homer, is the wearisome anguish of a guest who cannot escape an overgenerous host.

Ironically enough, it is Menelaus himself who best describes the dilemma to us. After Telemachus requests a speedy departure, Menelaus responds:

Telemachus, I for my part never will long detain you
here when you strain for home. I would disapprove of another
hospitable man who was excessive in friendship,
as of one excessive in hate. In all things balance is better.
It is equally bad when one speeds on the guest unwilling
to go, and when he holds back one who is hastening. Rather
one should befriend the guest who is there, but speed him when
    he wishes.

XV. 68–74

The irony, of course, lies in the fact that the very next words out of Menelaus' mouth are "Yet stay," because he wants to give him gifts and feast him properly before allowing him to leave. And while this would be only a minor delay, Menelaus also suggests that Telemachus accompany the king as they explore all of Greece together so that they can pursue presents. It is as if Menelaus has already forgotten the lengthy speech he just delivered.

Study Questions

1. To what danger does Athene alert Telemachus when she appears to him?

2. How does Helen read the portent of the eagle and the goose?

3. What does Telemachus request of Peisistratus as they approach Pylus?

4. Why does Theoclymenus wish to accompany Telemachus on his journey home?

5. In what way does Odysseus again test Eumaeus?

6. What was the swineherd's status before he was a servant?

7. What changed that situation?

8. What happened to the Phoenician bondswoman in Eumaeus' story?

9. What does Theoclymenus do that prompts Telemachus to change his mind concerning where the prophet will stay in Ithaca?

10. Where does Telemachus go after leaving his ship?

Answers

1. She alerts him to the suitors' ambush.

2. She reads it as a sign of Odysseus' imminent vengeance against the suitors.

3. He asks Peisistratus to help him avoid Nestor.

4. He is a fugitive for killing a man in Argos.

5. He tells Eumaeus that he intends to beg in the city.

6. He was a prince of the isle of Syria.

7. He was kidnapped by Phoenician traders and sold into sla-
    very.

8. She died on board the ship before reaching her homeland.

9. He reads a portent in favor of Telemachus' family.

10. Telemachus goes to Eumaeus' shelter.

Suggested Essay Topic

Consider the present status of Eumaeus the swineherd. What
new dimensions are added to his character by his life story? In what
ways is he similar to the Phoenician slave? In what ways does he
differ from her? What is significant about these similarities and
differences? What is Homer trying to say about the status and duties of household slaves in the Greek world of his day?

Book XVI

New Character:

Amphinomus: *the least violent of the suitors*

Summary

Telemachus enters the dwelling of Eumaeus as the swineherd
and Odysseus take their morning meal. Eumaeus, overjoyed to see
Telemachus safely returned to Ithaca, embraces his master and
weeps tears of joy. Telemachus questions Eumaeus about his guest,
and the swineherd explains Odysseus' fictional situation.
Telemachus agrees to send the guest where he desires to go, but
admits that present circumstances prohibit him from entertaining his guest at his own hall.

Telemachus sends Eumaeus off to secretly tell Penelope of her
son's return and relieve her of her fears. However, after Eumaeus
has departed for the city, Athene appears to Odysseus and beck-
ons him outside. Changing him back to his original, vibrant self,
she commands him to reveal himself to his son. Odysseus enters
the house, and Telemachus, in awe of his sudden change, believes

him to be a god. Odysseus spends some time convincing Telemachus that he is his father, but once he has persuaded his son of his identity, the two break down and tearfully rejoice for quite some time. When they have finished their long lament, they begin planning the death of the suitors. Telemachus details the great numbers of the suitors to Odysseus, who believes that Zeus and Athene will support them against the incalculable odds.

Meanwhile, Telemachus' companions return to the city and send a herald to inform Penelope of her son's return. Eumaeus meets the herald on his way to Penelope's chamber, and while the swineherd delivers Telemachus' message to Penelope privately, the herald's proclamation reaches the ears of the suitors.

The suitors despair over the failure of their plan, and when they have rejoined those of their number who had gone to perform the ambush, the large group meets at the place of assembly. There Antinoös, fearing the repercussions of their plot when it becomes known to the Ithacans, suggests they find and murder Telemachus immediately. Amphinomus, one of the chief suitors, is able to dissuade the suitors from taking this course of action. He suggests that if the gods themselves have delivered Telemachus from their hands, they had best give up the plot. The suitors agree with Amphinomus.

They return to Odysseus' palace to resume their feasting but are interrupted by Penelope, who, having learned of her son's present safety, descends to the great hall to rebuke the plotting suitors. She centers on Antinoös, whose father had been rescued through the influence of Odysseus; now Antinoös repays Odysseus by plotting the death of the man's son. Eurymachus falsely reassures Penelope that he will personally see to the safety of

Telemachus among the suitors. Penelope returns to her chamber, where she weeps until drifting off to sleep.

Eumaeus returns to his shelter and informs Telemachus and Odysseus, who has since resumed his beggar disguise, that he has accomplished his assigned task. When Telemachus questions him regarding the return of the suitors from their ambush, Eumaeus tells him that he did indeed see a ship returning to the harbor that was heavily laden with weapons. Eumaeus' guests then eat their evening meal and retire for the evening.

Analysis

The revelation of identity is a motif that continually surfaces throughout the *Odyssey*. When Odysseus decides to reveal himself, he usually does so in a dramatic manner that draws a strong reaction from those he is addressing. For example, throughout the entirety of Books VII-VIII, Odysseus is entertained by the Phaeaceans, who remain ignorant of his identity. By the time he reveals himself, Demodocus has already sung two songs honoring the famous hero who devised the Trojan Horse. We can only imagine the Phaeaceans' reactions when, after a suitably long introduction to cause suspense, Odysseus begins his long tale with: "I am Odysseus son of Laertes, known before all men / for the study of crafty designs, and my fame goes up to the heavens" (IX. 19–21). It is no wonder that the Phaeaceans are awed by his tale. They had unknowingly invited a legend into their midst and entertained him for two days. How could they help but listen and be enthralled by this god-like being who has walked among them? Even their reaction is held in suspense for some time, until Odysseus finally breaks in the midst of his narrative: "So he spoke, and all of them stayed stricken to silence, / held in thrall by the story all through the shadowy chambers" (XI. 334–35).

Throughout Odysseus' recited narrative, he often reveals his identity at crucial moments in the plot. When he foolishly reveals himself to Polyphemus, he incurs the wrath of Poseidon. When he threatens Circe, it is she who reveals his identity, for Hermes prophesied her defeat long ago.

Therefore, when the long-awaited reunion between father and son occurs, we should already be anticipating a scene developing fully from the motif of the revealed identity. And we are not disappointed. Telemachus is awed by his father's presence, and he averts his gaze from this seemingly divine being. Telemachus does not instantly recognize his long lost father, as we might have expected. Odysseus must spend time persuading his son who he is, even after speaking those magic words which Telemachus must have only dreamed about ever hearing: "But I am your father, for whose sake you are always grieving / as you look for violence from others, and endure hardships" (XVI. 188–89).

Telemachus' denial at his point can only be amusing. Odysseus must continue: "Telemachus, it does not become you to wonder too much / at your own father when he is here, nor doubt him. No other / Odysseus than I will ever come back to you" (XVI. 202–204). Then, when the suspense and tension have at last lifted through Telemachus' acceptance of his father, we receive the tears and joyful reunion that we have been awaiting for sixteen chapters.

Study Questions

1. Why is Eumaeus so excited to see Telemachus?

2. Upon what errand does Telemachus send Eumaeus?

3. What prompts Odysseus to reveal his identity to Telemachus?

4. Why is Telemachus frightened by his father's appearance?

5. Whom does Odysseus assert will aid Telemachus and him in his struggle against the suitors?

6. With what part of Odysseus' plan does Telemachus disagree?

7. How do the suitors learn of Telemachus' return?

8. What prompts the suitors to disagree with Antinoös' proposal?

9. Of what does Eurymachus falsely reassure Penelope?

10. What suggests to Eumaeus that the suitors have returned from their failed ambush?

Answers

1. He had feared for Telemachus' life because of the suitors' proposed ambush.

2. Telemachus sends Eumaeus to inform Penelope of his return.

3. Athene tells Odysseus to do so.

4. He thinks Odysseus is a god.

5. Odysseus asserts that Athene and Zeus will assist.

6. Telemachus disagrees that they examine all the bondsmen serving Odysseus in Ithaca.

7. A herald from among Telemachus' companions announces his return.

8. Amphinomus dissuades them from going against the will of the gods.

9. Eurymachus falsely reassured Penelope that he will guard Telemachus against the suitors.

10. He saw a heavily armed ship put into the Ithacan port.

Suggested Essay Topic

Examine the three speeches given by suitors in Book XVI (Antinoös [364–392], Anphinomus [400–405], and Eurymachus [435–447]). Of what is each attempting to convince their audiences? What rhetorical strategies are employed by each to persuade their audiences? What do we learn about these characters from their respective speeches?

Book XVII

New Characters:

Melanthius: *a scornful goatherd*

Argos: *Odysseus' faithful old dog*

Eurynome: *Penelope's maidservant*

Summary

   In the morning, Telemachus leaves Eumaeus' dwelling and returns to the palace, where he is greeted warmly by his mother and the many servants who feared for his life. Telemachus commands his mother to vow sacrifices to the gods should their hardships be avenged. Penelope obeys, while Telemachus himself goes to the place of assembly. There Telemachus meets Peraeus with Theoclymenus the prophet. Telemachus tells Peraeus to hold onto his Spartan treasures until the conflict with the suitors is resolved. Telemachus then returns to his palace with Theoclymenus. Telemachus, Theoclymenus, and Penelope share a meal together, during which Theoclymenus reveals to Penelope the portent he had read to Telemachus the day before.

   Meanwhile, Odysseus and Eumaeus have headed towards the city at Telemachus' command. On their way there, they meet the scurrilous Melanthius the goatherd, who both verbally and physically abuses Odysseus. Odysseus holds his peace, struggling to control himself from slaying the goatherd. Unshaken by Eumaeus' curses, Melanthius leaves the two behind and enters the palace.

   When Odysseus and Eumaeus arrive at the palace, where the disguised beggar is supposed to beg his supper, they see the old dog, Argos, lying atop a heap of dung. This dog, which Odysseus left behind in its prime, is now a most pitiful creature, covered with ticks and barely able to move. Yet, recognizing Odysseus, the dog wags its tail and lays back its ears in a show of its loyalty. The wretched dog soon dies, having met its master again after twenty years of separation.

   Eumaeus enters the palace, shortly followed by Odysseus. Telemachus gives his disguised father a meal and commands him to beg from among the suitors. All the suitors pity him but Antinoös

who, gently provoked by the disguised beggar, throws a footstool at Odysseus, who walks away in silent bitterness. Penelope summons Odysseus to her presence, for she wishes to question him concerning his travels. Eumaeus tries to dissuade her from the interview, telling her that the man has indeed claimed to have heard news of Odysseus but that he is like so many other storytellers who have told her similar information. Nonetheless, Penelope wishes to speak to him, although, at Odysseus' suggestion, she agrees to wait until after the suitors have departed for the evening. Eumaeus, having served as messenger between Odysseus and Penelope, finally takes his leave of Telemachus and heads back to his shelter; Telemachus commands him, however, to return in the morning.

Analysis

Now that Odysseus has appeared before the larger Ithacan community in disguise, there is more room for the dramatic irony that fills many of the verses of the *Odyssey*. We see this notably during the Melanthius episode. Although Odysseus holds his peace after Melanthius' attack, Eumaeus calls upon the gods to return Odysseus to his home so that he can punish the scornful goatherd. Melanthius' response is suitably ironic:

> Shame on the speaking of this nasty-minded dog. Some day
> I will get him aboard a strong-benched ship, and take him
> far from Ithaca, where he could win me a good livelihood.
> If only Apollo, silver-bowed, would strike down Telemachos
> today in his halls, or he were killed by the suitors, as surely
> as Odysseus, far away, has lost his day of homecoming.
>
> XVII. 247–53

Melanthius, a loyal follower of the suitors, knows the power that will be his when Telemachus is eliminated. His own vow, of course, recoils back upon him. Melanthius wishes that Telemachus may suffer death as surely as Odysseus himself has already done so. The irony lies in the fact that Melanthius' vow is fulfilled, only not in the way he had intended. Odysseus himself has not died, and is in fact standing right there. Therefore, as surely as Odysseus has not died, so too will Telemachus not die. Melanthius has unwittingly stated the truth.

We see a similar use of irony later, after Antinoös strikes Odysseus with the footstool. Only this time, no one specifically mentions the long-lost Odysseus. Instead, the suitors remark:

> Antinoös, you did badly to hit the unhappy vagabond:
> a curse on you, if he turns out to be some god from heaven.
> For the gods do take on all sorts of transformations, appearing

as strangers from elsewhere, and thus they range at large through
the cities,
watching to see which men keep the laws, and which are violent.

XVII. 483–87

Of course, we know Odysseus is not a god. But the gods have indeed disguised him for the very reason which the suitors suggest:
to test them and to see which are righteous and which malevolent.
It is also appropriate that Odysseus' disguise makes others liken
him once more to a god. Yet this time the situation is reversed.
Before, Telemachus thought Odysseus a god for removing his disguise. Now, the suitors consider the possibility due to the lowly
appearance of the disguise itself, not because of the majesty with
which the gods envelop him when he stands revealed in his true
form.

Study Questions

1. Why does Telemachus tell Peraeus to hold onto Menelaus'
   presents?

2. What does Theoclymenus promise Penelope?

3. Whom does Eumaeus call upon to grant Odysseus' homecoming and the subsequent destruction of Melanthius?

4. Why does the dog Argos react to Odysseus' presence?

5. What is ironic about Athene's desire to have Odysseus test
   the suitors?

6. According to Antinoös, why do the other suitors give so freely
   to Odysseus?

7. Why does Penelope wish to see the disguised Odysseus?

8. Why does Eumaeus wish to dissuade Penelope of the interview?

9. Why does Odysseus suggest the interview be postponed until
   later?

10. What command does Telemachus issue to Eumaeus before
    the swineherd departs?

Answers

1. He fears the suitors will despoil him of his prizes.

2. Theoclymenus promises Penelope that Odysseus' return and vengeance are imminent

3. Eumaeus calls upon the nymphs, who are daughters of Zeus

4. He used to be Odysseus' own dog before his master left for Troy.

5. She has no intention of sparing any of them.

6. They generously donate food that does not belong to them.

7. She wants to hear possible news of Odysseus

8. He does not want her to believe what he thinks are the stranger's false assertions concerning Odysseus.

9. The violent suitors might disrupt the interview.

10. He tells the swineherd to return the next day.

Suggested Essay Topic

In Book XVII, we see once more a contrast between Eumaeus, the model servant, and the other, disloyal servants. In what ways do Melanthius and other servants casually referred to in the narrative differ from Eumaeus? What is the significance of Eumaeus' own commentary on the matter? What does Homer imply through his treatment of servants in Book XVII?

Book XVIII

New Characters:

Iros: *a quarrelsome beggar*

Melantho: *an unkind maidservant*

Summary

After Eumaeus has left, an angry beggar nicknamed Iros approaches the palace and threatens Odysseus with bodily harm should he fail to leave the place immediately. Odysseus resists the overbearing vagabond, and the suitors entertain themselves with the conflict. They set up a contest between the two of them, and Odysseus quickly knocks his fellow out and drags him away through the courtyard, much to the delight of the suitors.

The scandalous affair is not lost on Penelope, who is angry that the stranger should be so mistreated in her house. She decides to approach the suitors, but before she does so, Athene wraps her in a pleasant sleep that greatly enhances the queen's beauty. When Penelope descends with her handmaidens, the suitors are enraptured with her glorious visage, and Eurymachus compliments her beauty ardently. Penelope takes advantage of the moment to entice the suitors and coerce more presents out of them, a guileful act not lost on her admiring husband. The suitors quickly comply by sending their heralds out for more presents, and Penelope returns to her upper chamber bearing luxurious gifts.

The suitors continue their feasting into the evening hours, and they set up lights throughout the room. Odysseus suggests to the maidservants who are tending the fires that they withdraw to the upper chamber to keep Penelope company while he personally mans the fires. The maidens ridicule the disguised Odysseus at his suggestion, but he snaps back at them fiercely and they flee from him terrified.

Eurymachus begins directing harsh comments toward Odysseus, implying that the beggar would much prefer to beg than put in an honest day's work. Odysseus responds that he could outperform Eurymachus in any task, given the opportunity. Angered, Eurymachus hurls a footstool at Odysseus, who quickly ducks behind Amphinomus. The stool goes wild and wounds a cupbearer.

The suitors are outwardly bitter concerning the disruption of their customary festivities. Telemachus attempts to silence them, but this only angers them more. Amphinomus, however, is able to bring about a swift reconciliation and commands the suitors to drink some wine and return to their houses. The suitors agree to his advice and leave the palace for the evening.

Analysis

We see more dramatic irony surrounding Odysseus' presence among the suitors. When he has triumphed over Iros, the suitors toast him, saying:

> May Zeus, stranger, and all the other immortals give you
> what you want most of all and what is dear to your spirit,

for having stopped the wandering of this greedy creature
in our neighborhood.

XVIII. 112–15

Of course, what Odysseus wants "most of all" is the death and de-
struction of the suitors, so it is amusing to hear these words come
from the suitors themselves. Indeed, the irony is not lost on
Odysseus himself, for "great Odysseus was pleased at the omen."
The irony of the situation is akin to a message from the gods in
Odysseus' perception

The character of Amphinomus is developed further in Book
XVIII. The peace-keeping tendencies he exhibited during the assembly in Book XVI are proven sincere during the scenes which
take place in Odysseus' palace. He offers kind words to Odysseus
the beggar and prevents a bad situation from getting worse as ten-
sions rise toward the chapter's end. We might even view
Amphinomus as a tragic hero of sorts, for his kindliness, which had
not gone unrecognized by Penelope herself, cannot rescue him
from the fate appointed him. The reason for this, of course, is that
the company and cause he supports has been slated for destruction by the gods themselves. Athene sends Odysseus to review the
suitors but has no intention of sparing any of them. Odysseus attempts to warn Amphinomus to flee the coming slaughter, but the
man's fate is already predetermined, and there is nothing he can
do to avoid it, despite the grim foreboding he experiences at
Odysseus' words:

> . . . [Amphinomos] went back across the room, heart saddened
> within him,
> shaking his head, for in his spirit he saw the evil,
> but still could not escape his doom, for Athene had bound him
> fast, to be strongly killed by the hands and spear of Telemachos.

XVIII. 153–56

Amphinomus is a victim of predestination, cursed with an innate
sense of his doom, but "bound" securely by the will of the gods to
receive his punishment for accompanying the suitors. The man
who saved Telemachus' life through persuasive pacifism will die a
violent death at the point of his beneficiary's spear.

Study Questions

1. Why does Iros want to expel Odysseus from the palace?
2. Why does he begin trembling before the fight?
3. What advice is given vainly to Penelope by Eurynome?
4. What does Athene do about Penelope's refusal?
5. How do the suitors react to the goddess's actions towards Penelope?
6. What does Penelope prompt the suitors to do when she speaks to them?
7. In what way does Odysseus threaten the maidservants?
8. How does Odysseus respond to Eurymachus' slanderous insults?
9. Whom does Eurymachus hit with the footstool?
10. What calms the suitors down at the end of Book XVIII?

Answers

1. He is competition for the other beggar.
2. Odysseus reveals his sinews.
3. She advises Penelope to wash herself before appearing before the suitors
4. She drifts Penelope into a sleep that enhances her beauty.
5. They are enthralled by her beauty.
6. Penelope prompts them to bring her more gifts.
7. Odysseus threatens to tell Telemachus of their behavior.
8. He suggests that he can outdo Eurymachus at any task.
9. He hits a random cupbearer with the footstool.
10. They are calmed by Amphinomus' words.

Suggested Essay Topic

In Book II, Antinoös made angry allegations concerning

Penelope's deceitful behavior. How do the events of Book XVIII support his suspicions? Why does Odysseus react as he does to Penelope's actions? How do we better understand the relationship between Odysseus and Penelope through the events of this chapter? What is Homer's attitude toward Penelope's behavior? In what way does the poet want his audience to perceive her?

Book XIX

Summary

After the suitors have departed, Odysseus and Telemachus remove the weapons and armor from the great hall and stow them in the upper chamber of the palace. Telemachus retires to his room, but Odysseus remains in the great hall until Penelope arrives and sits with him before a roaring fire. She questions him as to his name and country. When he initially attempts to avoid the issue, she leads the conversation by relating her own situation among the suitors and her attempt to stall them for as long as possible. When she again requests his identity, he tells her his name is Aethon from Crete. Altering the story he told Eumaeus significantly, he claims to be the younger brother of the famous Cretan prince, Idomeneus. When his older brother departed for Troy, "Aethon" remained behind in Crete. There he had the opportunity to entertain the traveling Odysseus for twelve days because the Ithacan had encountered stormy weather on his way to Troy.

Penelope is moved by his story but demands proof of its authenticity by asking her guest to describe Odysseus' clothing and appearance. Odysseus cleverly describes a mantle and golden clasp that Penelope herself had given him. Penelope no longer doubts his tales, so Odysseus tells her that her husband is in Thesprotia and possesses the means to return soon to his household. Although Penelope wishes to believe him, she doubts that she will ever be rejoined with her long absent husband.

Nevertheless, she offers to have her guest washed and bedded for the evening, but Odysseus refuses a bed and says he will accept a footbath only from an older woman whose heart has known the

same sorrow that he has experienced. Penelope summons Eurycleia, who gladly offers to tend the stranger whom she claims reminds her so strongly of her long lost master.

However, as Eurycleia examines his leg, she notices a scar that Odysseus had received as a boy when visiting his maternal grandfather, Autolycus. Odysseus had been hunting with Autolycus' sons on Mount Parnassus during a visit to receive promised gifts from his grandfather, who had named Odysseus and suggested the visit years earlier. Now Odysseus was hunting a wild boar, and presently engaged the beast at close quarters. Although slaying the beast, Odysseus received a leg wound, just above his knee. His grandfather's family brought him to the house and healed him, and then sent him home bearing many gifts. Odysseus then related the story to his family and household.

Now, when Eurycleia realizes who sits before her, she is over-joyed and drops Odysseus' foot into the water basin, tipping it over and spilling the water. She turns to inform Penelope, but her mistress is kept distracted by Athene. Odysseus quickly grabs his nurse by the throat and commands her to keep her mouth quiet. Eurycleia obeys her master and contains her excitement, running to fetch another water basin to finish bathing his feet.

Penelope next relates a curious dream of hers to Odysseus. She dreamt that twenty geese were eating in her house when an eagle swooped down and slaughtered them. While she wept for the slain geese, the eagle returned and claimed to be Odysseus, who had returned to slay the suitors, who were represented in the dream as geese.

However, Penelope believes this seemingly prophetic dream to be a false one. Resigning herself to her fate as a future wife of one of the suitors, she tells Odysseus that she will give herself away at last the next day. She will set up twelve axes, as Odysseus himself used to do, and command the suitors to string Odysseus' mighty bow and shoot an arrow straight through the assembled axe handles. The one who succeeds at the trial shall claim Penelope for his own. Odysseus encourages her to institute the contest, claiming that Odysseus himself will return before the suitors accomplish the difficult feat.

Although pleased by Odysseus' speech, Penelope admits that the hour for sleeping is upon her. She climbs to her upper chamber and falls to sleep with the aid of Athene.

Analysis

The exchange between Eurycleia and Odysseus concerning the latter's scar is a famous one. The interpolated story of the origin of Odysseus' scar certainly causes suspense as we are forced to wait for Eurycleia's reaction to her discovery. This suspense began when Eurycleia suggested the similarity between Odysseus and his beggar persona. Because no one else had previously made this observation, her statement was a foreshadowing of the recognition scene to come.

Then, at the moment of realization, the narrator suddenly leaves the immediate time frame of the narrative and pulls us into the distant past. Scholars have recognized how this scene exemplifies a feature of Homeric narrative: the eternal present of the narration[2]. No matter whether we are witnessing events that take place during the main timeline of the *Odyssey* (which occupies little more than a fortnight) or flashbacks from decades earlier, we always derive a sense of immediacy from the narration.

What is most remarkable about this particular "flashback" is that the narrator himself offers us the story and does not filter the past narrative through the speech or thoughts of another character, which is usually the case with most of the past narratives presented in the *Odyssey*. We are simply asked to forget about the present and enter the past as if the present we just witnessed had never yet occurred. For example, as critics have noted, one moment we see Eurycleia the old nurse preparing to wash the feet of her middle-aged charge, and the next instant we see her laying the baby Odysseus in the arms of his grandfather, Autolycus. We are no longer conscious of the forty or so years that have since passed away; those decades have vanished completely from our perception. Then, after we have been given a sense of temporal perspective by the chronologically early narrative, we are suddenly yanked back into that other present, years later, when Eurycleia drops Odysseus' foot to the ground in utter amazement.

Study Questions

1. What action is taken by Odysseus and Telemachus after the suitors depart?

2. Who scorns Odysseus for the second time when she sees him in the great hall?

3. When does Odysseus' persona claim to have entertained Odysseus in Crete?

4. How does Odysseus seem to authenticate his story?

5. What does he suggest about Odysseus' homecoming?

6. Why does Eurycleia feel sympathy for Odysseus' persona?

---

2.   This theory was introduced by Erich Auerbach in the opening chapter of his *Mimesis*.

7. How did Odysseus receive his name?

8. What inflicted him with the wound that formed his scar?

9. How is Odysseus represented in Penelope's dream?

10. How does she propose to choose her husband from among the suitors?

Answers

1. They hide the weapons and armor from the great hall.

2. Odysseus is scorned by Melantho.

3. Odysseus' persona claims to have entertained him on Odysseus' way to Troy.

4. He describes Odysseus' attire and personal servant perfectly.

5. Odysseus will journey to Ithaca from Thesprotia shortly.

6. His bad fortune reminds her of Odysseus.

7. His grandfather, Autolycus, named him "distasteful."

8. The scar was inflicted by a wild boar

9. He appears as an avenging eagle.

10. She will choose him through the contest of the bow.

Suggested Essay Topic

Analyze Penelope's dream of the eagle and the geese. What links the imagery in the dream with other symbols in the *Odyssey*? What is curious about Penelope's attitude toward the geese in the dream? What do her actions in the dream seem to suggest? What is odd about her request to have Odysseus interpret the dream? What is ironic about their discussion of the dream?

Book XX

New Characters:

Philoitius: *a loyal oxherd*

Agelaus: *a chief suitor*

Summary

Odysseus beds down on the floor but is soon bothered by the noise of the disloyal maidservants fleeing the palace to make love to the suitors. Odysseus feels the urge to destroy them on the instant but eventually gains control of himself and lets them go for the moment. He then suffers a night of anxiety and restlessness. He fears that he will be unable to defeat the suitors due to their overwhelming numbers. Athene descends from Olympus, however, and reassures him that with her aid, he is able to accomplish virtually anything. She then drifts him off into a peaceful sleep. Just as Odysseus falls asleep, Penelope awakes torn by doubt concerning her decision to marry one of the suitors. She wishes the gods would carry her off in a stormwind and deposit her in the land of the dead, where she might be reunited with Odysseus at last. Just so, she recalls, did the gods destroy the unmarried daughters of Pandareus.

Dawn arrives, and Odysseus begs Zeus for signs of success. The storm god replies with a peal of thunder in a cloudless sky. Odysseus also overhears a young maid wishing the thunder is a sign that this will be the last feast celebrated by the suitors. Odysseus gladly welcomes these favorable portents.

Meanwhile, Eurycleia commands the many household servants to ready for the day's feasting, which will begin early because the day is a public festival. Eumaeus arrives and greets Odysseus warmly, but Melanthius arrives and verbally abuses the disguised stranger once more. Philoitius the cowherd also arrives, having ferried over the livestock he tends for Odysseus on the isle of Cephallenia. Philoitius treats Odysseus kindly and expresses his loyalty for the master whom he hopes will one day return to Ithaca.

The suitors arrive and begin their feasting, waited upon by the herdsmen, Eumaeus, Philoitius, and Melanthius. Telemachus sets a place for Odysseus and commands the suitors to behave themselves and not abuse the stranger. In spite of his warning, a brash suitor named Ctesippus throws an ox hoof at Odysseus, who neatly dodges it. Telemachus rebukes him, only to rouse the anger of the suitors. Another suitor named Agelaus attempts to calm down the group, but demands that Telemachus resolve the conflict by bestowing his mother on one of them. Telemachus asserts that he has suggested previously to his mother to marry, but that he dreads asking her to leave against her will.

At that moment, the suitors are possessed by an uncontrollable hysteria. They laugh wildly with a will not their own. Theoclymenus interprets this as a dark omen, but Eurymachus mocks him severely. Theoclymenus stalks out of the palace in a dark mood and rejoins the benevolent Peraeus. The suitors continue to mock Telemachus, telling him that he should ship his useless guests off to Sicily to be slaves. Penelope, in the meantime, has set up a chair outside the room and listens to the hall's revelry which is destined to end in violence.

Analysis

Scholars have noted the significance of Book XX: it sets the stage for the final act of the *Odyssey*: Odysseus' and Telemachus' revenge against the suitors. The scene appropriately reintroduces almost every major character on Ithaca: Amphinomus, Antinoös, Eurymachus, Theoclymenus, Eumaeus, Melanthius, Eurycleia, as well as the family of Odysseus, Telemachus, and Penelope. We also see the arrival of Philoitius, who will be a major figure in the scenes ahead.

A theme profoundly emphasized in these scenes is that of Telemachus' coming into manhood. As we have seen in previous scenes, Telemachus has become increasingly bolder in the suitors' presence, and they are just as astonished with each occurrence. He makes his boldest statement to them after their arrival that day:

> . . . This house does not belong to the people,
> but it belongs to Odysseus; he acquired it; this makes it
> mine, and so, you suitors, hold back your spirit for insults
> and blows, or else there may be a quarrel and fight between us.
> XX. 264–67

As might be expected, the suitors again "bit their lips in amazement / at Telemachos, and the daring way he had spoken to them" (268–69).

His transition from the passive dreamer he had been at the poem's beginning to the active figure of authority he has become is noticed by Telemachus himself. He notes this change in himself when he rebukes Ctesippus: "Let none display any rudeness / here in my house. I now notice all and know of it, better / and worse alike, but before now I was only an infant" (308–310). In this way, spurred on initially by Athene and then by Odysseus, Telemachus lets us know that he is ready for the bloody rite of passage to manhood that will take place in the violent scenes to come.

Study Questions

1. Why is Odysseus pensive throughout the long night?

2. Why is he finally able to fall asleep?

3. What does Penelope fervently long for in her hopeless anxiety?

4. Why does Eurycleia hurry the servants more emphatically than usual?

5. What decision made by Philoitius proves his loyalty to Odysseus?

6. What is the "gift" bestowed upon Odysseus by Ctesippus?

7. How does Telemachus answer Agelaus concerning Penelope's decision?

8. What is unusual about the suitors' sudden laughter?

9. How does Theoclymenus interpret it?

10. What do the suitors suggest Telemachus do with Odysseus and Theoclymenus?

Answers

1. He doubts his ability both to defeat the suitors and to survive the consequences of the act.

2. Athene reassures him.

3. She hopes for death

4. The day celebrates a public festival.

5. Philoitius decides to keep his oxen in Odysseus' service rather than seek out a new liege

6. Ctesippus bestows upon Odysseus an ox's hoof.

7. He tells Agelaus that he tries to persuade Penelope to marry one of them, but he refuses to force her to do so.

8. It is divinely inspired.

9. He sees it as a mark of darkness and doom.

10. They suggest that Odysseus and Theoclymenus be shipped off to be sold as slaves.

Suggested Essay Topic

With the arrival of Philoitius we have another perspective on the role of the loyal servant. Examine Philoitius' speeches to Odysseus. What do we learn about his character through his stories? What are the options he has to consider? What is significant about each of his options? What makes his decision so crucial to Odysseus' assessment of his loyalty?

Book XXI

New Character:

Leodes: *a suitor who serves as a diviner to his companions*

Summary

Penelope ascends to the upper chamber of the palace where Odysseus' famous bow is kept. Odysseus had received the mighty weapon years ago from Iphitus, a friend whom he met shortly before Iphitus' death at the hands of Heracles. Odysseus had kept the bow in Ithaca when he left for Troy. Now Penelope retrieves the bow, its arrows, and her husband's strong axes. She brings them down into the main hall and offers her challenge to the suitors: whoever strings the bow and shoots an arrow through twelve axe handles may claim Penelope as his bride. Antinoös, though out-wardly cautious, believes that he will be the one to accomplish the feat.

Telemachus astonishes the suitors by expertly setting up the axes in a perfect row; he had never before seen them set up in this way. Claiming that his mother will be freed from her obligation to remarry if he can accomplish the feat, Telemachus is the first to attempt to string the bow. After failing three times, Telemachus almost succeeds in stringing the bow, but a quick sign from his disguised father makes him surrender at the last moment.

The suitors, at Antinoös' bidding, take turns attempting to string the bow. The first to try after Telemachus is the prophet Leodes, who fails to string the bow. Anguished, he announces that death is preferable to losing the goal for which they have all striven so long; surely such death awaits all those who fail in the contest. Antinoös quiets him down and then orders Melanthius to start a fire and bring tallow to limber up the stiff bow. The goatherd com-plies, and the suitors resume their attempts at the bow, but to no avail.

Eumaeus and Philoitius wander outside the hall, and Odysseus shortly follows them. After ascertaining the extent of their loyalty, Odysseus suddenly reveals his identity to them, proving his authen-ticity with the scar on his leg. Eumaeus and Philoitius tearfully re-joice, agreeing to aid Odysseus in his vengeance against the suitors. After Odysseus has given them their orders, the three return in-side, where Eurymachus himself has at last picked up the bow. He also fails to string the weapon and mourns not so much the loss of Penelope but the realization of the suitors' complete inferiority to the bow's master. However, Antinoös superstitiously uses the holi-day as an excuse for their failures. He suggests that the suitors sac-rifice goats to Apollo the next day and then attempt once more to win Penelope's contest.

It is at this moment that Odysseus requests to try the bow in order to see if he has retained the strength of his youth. Antinoös violently protests, telling him to sit down and be silent, or else they will ship him off to be mutilated by ruthless kings. Penelope mocks Antinoös' scorn, suggesting they let the beggar make the attempt. She asserts that the stranger cannot win her in marriage and that

he only wants to try the bow for personal reasons. Eurymachus admits, however, that it is not the suitors' fear that the beggar will win Penelope. They dread the scandalous reproaches they will receive if the old man succeeds where they have failed. Penelope continues to mock the suitors, but Telemachus takes the opportunity to silence her and send her away to her upper chamber. Although startled by his brashness, Penelope obeys and retreats to her room, where Athene sends her into a deep sleep. Now she is safely out of the way for the events to come.

Eumaeus, following Odysseus' plans, picks up the bow and starts carrying it toward his master. The suitors immediately start threatening him, and the swineherd, daunted by them, returns the bow to its place. Telemachus, however, recovers the situation by offering Eumaeus some threats of his own. His angry speech makes the suitors laugh, and while their mood is lightened, Eumaeus takes the opportunity to bring the bow to Odysseus. The swineherd, following his orders, then commands Eurycleia to bar the doors to the hall and to leave them closed no matter what clamor she hears within. Philoitius uses a strong cord to tie up the doors to the outer courtyard; he then returns to the great hall, the doors of which are barred behind him by Eurycleia.

Odysseus sizes up the bow, examining it deftly from all angles and sides; the suitors are amazed at his expertise. He then proceeds to string the bow as easily as a musician strings his lyre. He plucks the string to test its resonance, and the suitors are astounded. Drawing a swift arrow from the quiver, he launches the shaft through all twelve axe handles without even rising from his chair. At a nod from Odysseus, Telemachus rises, takes a firm hold of his weapons, and stands beside his noble father.

Analysis

A psychoanalytic reading of Book XXI yields insight into a complex conflict between Telemachus and Odysseus that exists beneath the surface of the narrative. Telemachus, who has now grown to manhood, manifests his maturity by asserting authority not only over the suitors, but also over his mother. Now that he has come of age, Telemachus has also expressed his desire many times to gain control over his household, as befits the son of a powerful man who has perished. However, what those whom Telemachus addresses do not know is that Odysseus is indeed alive. Therefore, Telemachus assumes his manhood in an environment that is not yet able to sustain his mastery. When Odysseus resolves his troubles in Ithaca, we must assume that he, and not Telemachus, will once again become the master in his house.

The tension for control of Odysseus' house is present, at least symbolically, between father and son. We see this metaphorically in the contest of the bow. Odysseus' bow is a symbol of phallic power which the suitors attempt to master and control. If they can bend the bow to their will, then Penelope, the female counterpart to the bow, will be theirs to control as well.

We should therefore experience no small surprise to see Telemachus taking part in the contest. Surely this is a competition between Odysseus and the men who have come to usurp his bride; Odysseus' son is certainly unsuitable for this game. Yet Telemachus does indeed take part, and his reasons should make us at least a little uncomfortable:

> I myself am also willing to attempt the bow. Then,
> if I can put the string on it and shoot through the iron,
> my queenly mother would not go off with another, and leave me
> sorrowing here in the house; since I would still be found here
> as one now able to take up his father's glorious prizes.
>
> XXI. 113–117

Those "glorious prizes," we must assume, can only include Penelope, the ultimate prize in this competition. The Oedipal implications are obvious. It is not that Telemachus consciously desires to wed his mother. After all, Telemachus knows at this point that, competition or no, Odysseus has returned and will shortly butcher the suitors no matter who strings his bow. However, Penelope's symbol as the power of the household is one which subconsciously attracts Telemachus. He desires to rule his house, preferably with his mother at his side.

And the irony of the situation is that Telemachus nearly does succeed in stringing the bow. After three strained attempts, he nearly bends the bow to his will. But Odysseus is not blind to the implications of this contest. For this reason, more than any other perhaps, he signals his son to give over the competition. Only the father may control the phallic symbol of authority in the household. When Odysseus has passed away, then will his son gain that authority. And Telemachus, realizing somewhere deep within his consciousness that what he desires cannot be, gives in. He feigns failure and releases the bow at last, leaving it there for his father to pick up and wield once more. The subtle conflict, for now at least, has ended.

Study Questions

1. Why didn't Odysseus take his bow with him to Troy?

2. What were the two parts of Penelope's proposed competition?

3. Why are the suitors surprised at Telemachus' ability to set up the axes?

4. Why does Telemachus assert that he should take part in the competition?

5. What makes him fail?

6. What is Leodes' lament after he fails to string the bow?

7. How does Antinoös try to simplify the competition after Leodes' failure?

8. What most perturbs Eurymachus concerning his failure to string the bow?

9. Why is Eumaeus initially unable to bring Odysseus the bow?

10. What does Odysseus do immediately before stringing the bow?

Answers

1. It is a memorial to his friend, Iphitus.

2. The two parts are to string the bow and shoot an arrow through twelve axe handles

3. He had never before seen them set up in this way.

4. If he succeeds, his mother will be freed of her obligation to marry one of the suitors.

5. Odysseus signals him to fail at the last moment.

6. He longs for death now that he has failed in his courting of Penelope.

7. He commands Melanthius to start a fire to heat the bow and to bring fat to make it limber.

8. Their failure is a sign of Odysseus' absolute superiority over them.

9. He is daunted by the threats of the suitors.

10. He examines it scrupulously.

Suggested Essay Topic

Examine Penelope's contest in some detail. What is significant about the suitors' failure to string the bow? What is significant about their reactions to their own failures? Look particularly at the speeches made by Eurymachus, Leodes, and Penelope herself? How do these serve to make the competition of the utmost importance to all involved?

Book XXII

New Character:

Amphimedon: *a suitor who later describes his death to Agamemnon (in Book XXIV)*

Summary

Odysseus bounds from his chair and scatters his arrows on the floor beneath himself. He then lets another arrow fly straight into the throat of Antinoös. The suitors, amazed, believe Odysseus shot the man by accident and threaten to kill him for his carelessness. It is at this moment that Odysseus reveals his identity to them at last, and the men are deeply afraid of his wrath. Eurymachus tells Odysseus that the men will make restitution for their evil deeds, but the vengeful man will not be satisfied. Eurymachus then tries to lead the men in a charge to break past Odysseus to the door behind him, but the archer cuts him down swiftly.

Amphinomus charges against Odysseus, attempting to overbear him, but Telemachus casts his spear at the man with deadly accuracy. Then, obtaining his father's approval, Telemachus runs to the chamber containing the hidden weapons and draws out helmets, shields, and spears for his companions and himself. He quickly returns to Odysseus, and he and the two herdsmen quickly don the arms. Odysseus in the meantime propels his shafts with speed and vigor, killing a man with every arrow that leaves his bow.

When he has no arrows remaining, he dons the equipment that Telemachus has retrieved for him.

The suitor Agelaus tries to muster the other suitors together. Melanthius the goatherd assists them by slipping away from the room through a vent in the wall; he finds the equipment hidden by Telemachus and brings back twelve sets of arms and armor. The suitors quickly don these, but Telemachus spots Melanthius leaving the room to find more equipment. Odysseus sends the two herdsmen out to intercept Melanthius and hold him captive.

Eumaeus and Philoitius obey their master; they ambush and subdue the goatherd on his way out of the weapons chamber. They tie his arms and legs behind him and hoist him up to the roof rafters for painful safekeeping. The herdsmen then rejoin Odysseus and Telemachus. Athene appears in the likeness of Mentor to stand on the side of Odysseus. Agelaus threatens to slay Mentor's family if he does not abandon Odysseus to his fate. Athene then rebukes Odysseus for fearing to attack the armed suitors, despite their numbers, for he fought more vehemently on the plains of Troy than he does in his own home. She then changes her form to that of a swallow and flies up to the hall's rafters, unnoticed by the suitors.

Agelaus and the five suitors most adept at fighting lead the suitors in a charge. Athene causes their thrown spears to fly wildly from their marks, but Odysseus and his companions hurl their spears with lethal consequences for the suitors. The frightened suitors back away from the dead men, and Odysseus' party takes advantage of this to retrieve their spears from the fallen bodies. Six more spears thrown by the suitors miss their marks due to Athene's intervention, although Telemachus and Eumaeus sustain minor injuries. Again Odysseus' men throw their spears effectively, then use their second spears to engage the suitors in close melee.

Athene throws the suitors into a blind panic, and soon the four allies slaughter most all of them. Leodes leaps before Odysseus and demands mercy because he did not partake in the suitors' sinful practices. However, because Leodes is a suitor who meant to win Odysseus' wife while the latter was still alive, Odysseus shows him no mercy; the warrior picks up a stray sword and lops off the prophet's head. Phemius the bard also begs for mercy, claiming the suitors forced him to sing for them. Telemachus backs up his claim, adding that Medon the faithful herald should also be spared. Odysseus heeds his son and sends the two men out of the courtyard.

With the suitors dead, Odysseus summons Eurycleia and orders her to bring forth the maidservants who slept with the suitors. These women assist the fighters in carrying the corpses into the courtyard and washing the blood from the palace. After the palace is washed down, the twelve disloyal maidservants are gathered into the center of the courtyard and hung from a high column. Melanthius the goatherd is pulled down from his imprisonment and brutally mutilated. Telemachus and the herdsmen then cleanse themselves after their unclean work.

Odysseus next brings in brimstone and sulfur and uses them to sterilize the palace interior. Eurycleia then summons the loyal handmaidens, who greet Odysseus warmly and welcome him home.

Analysis

Homer offers us a very vivid and dark picture here at the poem's climactic moments. The suitors have at last suffered for their treatment of Odysseus' family and household, and the disloyal servants have likewise been punished for their conduct. But what we see is not a scene of glory untainted by the reality of mortal slaughter, but a harsh picture almost too terrible for us to bear. Indeed, Homer never glorified war in the *Iliad*, but showed us the baser side of every martial deed, whether it was a romantic duel or the mass slaughter of a company of sleeping soldiers.

So too are we forced to witness the stark grimness of the suitors' murder. Many scholars have condemned the treatment of the suitors, saying that their punishment was taken to extremes which did not fit their crimes. Yet, even if this is the case, we must not condemn Homer or his poem for Odysseus' treatment of the suitors. Homer does not judge the morality of the situation; he tells us a story and leaves it to his audience to judge the actions of his characters. Critics of Homer often admire his truly objective perspective. Whether he is describing women at a dance or men butchering their families, he uses the same pace, rhythm, imagery, and vocabulary. He truly presents us with the omnipotent, impartial narrator.

That impartiality, however, does not make his narrator distant or remote from the scene. On the contrary, we witness the beheading of a man begging for mercy on his knees. We see twelve women noosed simultaneously, and we see their feet struggle for a few moments before stiffening. We see another fellow tortured for hours before having his ears, nose, groin, hands, and feet cut off. Every action in the minutest detail is presented to us, but with no active commentary from the narrator. Does Homer's narrator condone the extent of Odysseus' brutality? If we could truly tell the narrator's opinion, his task would be a failure. Homer shows us the glorious and the lowly, the beautiful and the grotesque, the sublime and the pathetic. Each quality of his narrative, negative or positive, is given equal weight. Homer's world, like our own, is a place that presents us with many images, but refuses to interpret them for us.

Study Questions

1. Which suitor is the first to taste Odysseus' vengeance?

2. What offer is made by Eurymachus to stave off Odysseus' attack?

3. How do the suitors begin obtaining weapons and armor?

4. How does Odysseus put a stop to this?

5. How do Eumaeus and Philoitius imprison Melanthius?

6. Why are the suitors' spears unable to find their marks?

7. Why does Odysseus ignore Leodes' plea?

8. Whom does he spare from the slaughter?

9. Whom do Odysseus' men execute after destroying the suitors?

10. What does Odysseus use to sterilize his hall thoroughly?

Answers

1. Antinoös is the first to taste Odysseus' vengeance.

2. The suitors will recompense him for their crimes.

3. Melanthius retrieves the hidden equipment for them.

4. He sends Eumaeus and Philoitius to stop Melanthius.

5. They bind him and hoist him up to the roof rafters.

6. Athene diverts them.

7. As a diviner, Leodes must have prayed for Odysseus' long absence.

8. He spares Medon and Phemius.

9. They execute Melanthius and the disloyal maidservants

10. He uses brimstone and sulfur.

Suggested Essay Topic

Examine Homer's use of poetic justice in Book XXII. How do certain characters' deaths recall past incidents or foreshadowing presented earlier in the narrative? Analyze the deaths of Antinoös and Melanthius particularly. How do the manner of their deaths recall earlier episodes involving them? Also explore characters whose deaths seem inappropriate. To what extent are we meant to sympathize with characters whose deaths appear unjust (e.g. Leodes and Amphinomus)?

Book XXIII

Summary

Eurycleia, acting upon Odysseus' orders, ascends merrily up to Penelope's chamber and wakens her with the news of her husband's return and the suitors' destruction. But, believing her servant to have lost her wits, Penelope scolds the aged nurse for playing such a cruel jest on her. Eurycleia swears that what she has said is true, and she stakes her life on that truth. Penelope, however, is unconvinced, and thinks a god has entered her palace to punish the suitors.

Penelope enters the great hall and sits opposite Odysseus, staring at him inquisitively but saying nothing to him. Telemachus rebukes his mother for her obstinacy, but Odysseus silences his son and believes his wife's silence is due to his own shabby attire. Odysseus goes to bathe and dress himself in finery, but first he warns Telemachus of the danger they must now face from the suitors' avengers. Odysseus commands Telemachus, the herdsmen, and the faithful maidservants to perform music and dancing so as to fool the Ithacans into thinking Penelope has married one of the suitors.

When Odysseus has been restored to his godlike self, assisted by the charms of Athene, he again returns to Penelope. Yet Penelope is still reluctant to embrace him. Irritated, Odysseus commands a bed to be brought to him so that he can sleep alone in the great hall.

Penelope takes the opportunity to cleverly suggest that Odysseus' own bed be brought to him. When Odysseus hears the suggestion, he is outraged, for Odysseus constructed the bed she refers to from the lodged stump of an olive tree. A chamber was built around the bed, whose roots still clung to the soil beneath it. The very notion that this bed could be moved sends him into a tirade on the infamy of the deed. Of course, this clue is all Penelope needs to assure herself of Odysseus' authenticity, for only the two of them have ever seen this illustrious bed. Penelope embraces her husband firmly and weeps tears of rejoicing. She begs her husband's forgiveness for her long doubt, explaining her fear that an impostor would deceive her.

Odysseus and his wife sit enfolded in each other's arms for so long a time that Athene must delay the Dawn from its accustomed rising. Odysseus and Penelope finally enter their bedchamber, but not until after Odysseus has warned his wife of the trials that he still must face and the voyages he must undertake at the bidding of Teiresias.

The reunited pair engage in their pleasurable "old ritual." After they have consummated their reunion, they tell each other of the many trials and tribulations they have endured for two decades. Odysseus begins his tale with his raid on the Ciconian and continues until his arrival on Ithaca with the aid of the Phaeaceans. They

fall to sleep at last, and Athene finally releases the restrained Dawn to commence her duty. Odysseus rises and commands Penelope to withdraw to her upper chamber and avoid the suitors' families when they come to claim the bodies of their deceased kin. Odysseus himself dons his armor and weapons and commands Telemachus and the herdsmen to do likewise. The four of them leave the palace and depart from the city, concealed by the power of Athene as they travel toward Laertes' farm.

Analysis

The cleverness and prudence we witness once more in Penelope certainly make her the most appropriate wife for Odysseus. The reunion of husband and wife which the poem has so long anticipated is delayed once more by Penelope's doubt. But we should not be surprised that Homer has employed such a device to create suspense. The poet is a master at keeping our interest while holding our expectations at bay. Then, without warning, he launches the expected conclusion at an unexpected time. So what is predictable becomes unpredictable.

We waited for four books to get our first glimpse of the poem's hero, but, as critics have suggested, his character becomes so well established by others' references to him that we are already familiar with the character when he enters the poem in Book V. Similarly, we are told of Odysseus' ten years of wanderings and imprisonment. It seems as if his homecoming will be delayed indefinitely. Then, still a long way from home, the adventurer boards a magic ship and is suddenly home in a matter of hours.

But when he arrives, he is asleep. The scene of Odysseus kissing the soil of Ithaca which we have long anticipated is denied us because of Athene's illusory mischief. But, just when we have given up hope for such a spectacle, Athene suddenly lifts all illusions, and Odysseus, convinced at last of his homecoming, prostrates himself on his beloved soil much as we thought he might have.

Odysseus' refusal to acknowledge his homecoming until the last minute is paralleled neatly by Penelope's refusal to believe in his arrival. But, after Odysseus spends a seemingly pointless speech extolling the virtues of his elaborately crafted bed, we are unexpectedly surprised by Penelope thrusting herself tearfully at her husband. We receive the scene we so long had anticipated, but not until Homer thickens the tension considerably.

Study Questions

1. How does Penelope initially react to Eurycleia's announcement?

2. After she believes that the suitors have been slain, whom does Penelope believe has accomplished the task?

3. Why does Telemachus rebuke Penelope in the great hall?

4. For what reason does Odysseus initially believe Penelope doubts his authenticity?

5. What does he do to rectify the situation?

6. How does Odysseus stall the people from discovering the truth concerning the suitors?

7. What causes Penelope to accept Odysseus' identity?

8. What fear caused her to withhold her acknowledgement for so long?

9. What must Athene do to ensure Odysseus and Penelope have sufficient time together?

10. To what destination do Odysseus and the men journey at the end of Book XXIII?

Answers

1. She believes Eurycleia to be mad.

2. Penelope believes it was done by a god.

3. He does so because his mother is silent before Odysseus.

4. Odysseus thinks Penelope doubts him because of his shabby clothing

5. He bathes and puts on fresh attire.

6. He commands Telemachus and the servants to feign a celebration within the palace.

7. He inadvertently proves his authenticity by revealing his knowledge of their bed's unique nature.

8. She feared that an impostor would deceive her.

9. She stalls the Dawn from rising.

10. They journey to Laertes' estate.

Suggested Essay Topic

In what ways does Odysseus' revelation of his identity to Penelope differ from other such disclosures? In what ways is this occurrence similar to other scenes like it? Trace the motif of the revealed identity from Odysseus' announcement to the Phaeaceans all the way to Penelope in Book XXIII (and Laertes in Book XXIV). What makes each scene distinct from the others? What makes these distinctions significant?

Book XXIV

New Characters:

Laertes: *Odysseus' father*

Dolius: *an aged servant of Laertes*

Eupeithes: *the vengeful father of Antinoös*

Summary

Hermes leads the souls of the dead suitors down to Hades' realm. There, Agamemnon and Achilles have been discussing their deaths. Agamemnon envies Achilles, whose body was fought over by his companions, and whose funeral rites were grand and accompanied by great games as befits a dead hero. Agamemnon, on the contrary, died ignobly at the hands of his wife, Clytemnestra, and her lover, Aegisthus. As the suitors approach the gates of the Underworld, the surprised Greek heroes approach them. Agamemnon singles out Amphimedon, whose house he had visited long ago. The Greek commander asks the perished suitor to explain what force slaughtered so many noble specimens of man-

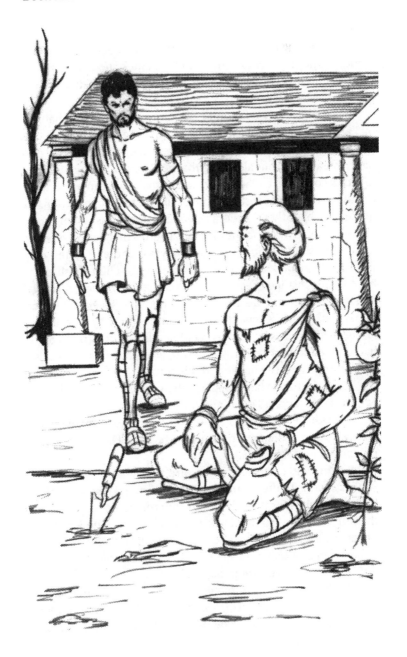

hood. Amphimedon then summarizes Odysseus' return to Ithaca and his subsequent revenge against the suitors. Agamemnon applauds Odysseus' great victory and Penelope's steadfastness, envying his friend's good fortune which differed so drastically from his own.

Meanwhile, Odysseus and his men reach the farm inhabited by Laertes; the estate is far removed from the main Ithacan city. Sending Telemachus and the two herdsmen into the house to prepare a meal, Odysseus alone approaches Laertes. Seeing his father in pitiful condition and working himself to the bone in his orchard, Odysseus decides to test his father's ability to recognize him. He first mocks his father's deplorable condition, then asks him to provide Odysseus' whereabouts. He tells Laertes that he had received Odysseus as a guest in his house five years earlier. Laertes, convinced his son has perished, begins mourning for him afresh, pouring dirt upon his aged head. Odysseus can stand the sight no longer and immediately reveals his identity to his father. Laertes is doubtful at first, but Odysseus proves his authenticity by showing his father his famous scar and by reciting a list of trees that Laertes had allotted to him years ago. Laertes, weeping tears of joy at the revelation, enters the house with his son.

There the others have prepared their meal, but before they can eat, the aged servant Dolius and his sons return from their labors to greet Odysseus. Amazed at his presence among them, Dolius' family welcomes their returned master heartily. The company then proceeds to eat their meal.

Meanwhile, rumor has gone forth to spread the news of the suitors' deaths to their families. The mourning kinsmen perform the funeral rites for their dead and ship the bodies of those from the surrounding islands back to their homes. The anguished Ithacans meet in assembly, and there Eupeithes, Antinoös' enraged father, suggests they punish Odysseus immediately for this horrible crime. However, Phemius and Medon arrive at the assembly to inform the Ithacans of the gods' participation in this struggle on the side of Odysseus. This speech, as well as further prophetic warnings by Halitherses, deters some of the Ithacans from taking arms against Odysseus.

However, more than half of the assembled Ithacans arm themselves and follow Eupeithes to battle. Odysseus and his company have finished their meal and await the coming of the angry islanders. Seeing their approach, the twelve of them (Odysseus, Telemachus, Laertes, Eumaeus, Philoitius, Dolius, and Dolius' six sons) ready their weapons and armor. The clash between the two factions is imminent, but Athene, up on Olympus, begs her father to allow a peaceful resolution to the conflict. Zeus complies wholeheartedly, and Athene descends from Olympus and appears to Odysseus' band in the shape of Mentor.

As Mentor, Athene stirs Laertes' courage and enhances his strength. The aged warrior hurls his spear at Eupeithes, felling him in a single blow. Odysseus and Telemachus dive into the crush of warriors, but before the fight can escalate, Athene stuns the Ithacan warriors and sends them fleeing in terror from the battlefield. Odysseus is eager to pursue them, but is stifled by a warning from Athene. Afterward, Athene, in the semblance of Mentor, harmonizes the two coalitions and establishes the prosperity and rulership of Odysseus among his people.

Analysis

Many of the themes that have run steadily through the *Odyssey* appropriately reach their conclusions in the poem's final chapter. This, above other considerations, must be the reason for Book XXIV's lengthy introduction in Hades' realm. There, from the lips of Agamemnon himself, we witness the fulfillment of the contrasting parallels that link the families of Odysseus and Agamemnon. When Agamemnon learns of Odysseus' success and Penelope's fidelity, he declares:

> O fortunate son of Laertes, Odysseus of many devices,
> surely you won yourself a wife endowed with great virtue.
> How good was proved the heart that is in blameless Penelope,
> Ikarios' daughter, and how well she remembered Odysseus,
> her wedded husband. Thereby the fame of her virtue shall never
> die away, but the immortals will make for the people
> of earth a thing of grace in the song for prudent Penelope.
> Not so did the daughter of Tyndareos fashion her evil

deeds, when she killed her wedded lord, and a song of loathing
will be hers among men, to make evil the reputation
of womankind, even for one whose acts are virtuous.

XXIV. 192–202

Here the contrasting functions of Penelope and Clytemnestra reach
their completion. Penelope is the perfect, loyal wife, and "the fame
of her virtue shall never / die away," while Clytemnestra's infamy
will live on as an example of the disloyal wife: "a song of loathing /
will be hers among men." While one might object to Homer's im-
plication that a wife is either a glorious heroine or a wicked sinner,
we must realize the true purpose for this distinction. Penelope and
Clytemnestra become archetypes for the extremes of nobility and
wretchedness in women. They are meant to be the unreal extremes
of fidelity and infidelity, and not entirely realistic figures. They
anachronistically become Platonic forms dwelling outside the reality of existence. This is not to say that Penelope is not without
her lovable, down-to-earth characteristics. However, the purpose
she serves is larger than what it appears to be at first glance.

The other motif that reaches a conclusion in Book XXIV is that
of the revealed identity. Seeing Laertes struggling voluntarily in his
orchard, Odysseus ponders deeply

whether to embrace his father and kiss him and tell him
everything, how he was come again to his own dear country,
or question him first about everything, and make trial of him.
In the division of his heart this way seemed best to him,
first to make trial of him and speak in words of mockery.

XXIV. 236–40

Odysseus' very hesitancy before assuming his disguise should hint
to us that there will be something different about this particular
scene of revelation. While the devious Odysseus is constantly considering options such as this one, he has never before done so to
determine whether or not he should mask his identity. The act was
always spontaneous, for, as Athene remarks in Book XIII, deception is a part of his "very nature."

The reason for Odysseus' initial uncertainty is the inherent
cruelty of casting a ruse on the suffering old man, whose love for

his son is indisputable. Just as we might have expected, Odysseus' fabrication inspires a rise of impassioned mourning on the part of his father:

> [Odysseus] spoke, and the black cloud of sorrow closed on Laertes.
> In both hands he caught up the grimy dust and poured it
> over his face and grizzled head, groaning incessantly.
> The spirit rose up in Odysseus, and now in his nostrils
> there was a shock of bitter force as he looked on his father.
> XXIV. 315–19

This was certainly not a reaction that Odysseus had anticipated. He regrets it deeply and immediately ends the ruse. It is appropriate that Odysseus' final deception leads to unpredictable results, for the master trickster had to learn that even his own cleverness has its limits. For, though he is godlike, Odysseus is only a mortal, and, well-traveled though he be, there is always much of the world that will remain beyond his grasp.

Study Questions

1. Who leads the suitors to Hades' realm?

2. Why does Agamemnon recognize Amphimedon?

3. In what activity is Laertes engaged when Odysseus finds him?

4. What decision must Odysseus make before approaching Laertes?

5. What reaction does he stir in his father?

6. What does Eupeithes suggest to the assembled Ithacans?

7. What news does Medon bring to the assembly?

8. What does Athene request of Zeus?

9. How is Laertes able to destroy Eupeithes?

10. What does Athene stop Odysseus from doing when the Ithacans flee from him?

Answers

1. Hermes leads them.

2. Agamemnon had once been a guest in his house.

3. Laertes is working laboriously in his orchard.

4. Odysseus must decide whether to tell Laertes the truth of his return or to deceive him

5. His father is struck by a severe fit of mourning

6. Eupeithes suggests that they attack Odysseus for his crimes

7. Medon brings news that that Odysseus' actions were favored by the immortals.

8. Athene asks Zeus to allow her to bring about a peaceful resolution to the Ithacan conflict

9. He is strengthened by Athene.

10. She stops Odysseus from pursuing them.

Suggested Essay Topic

Critics have noted the rather abrupt ending of the *Odyssey*. Do you think the finale of the poem is complete, or do there seem to be events missing? Explain your answer, drawing upon the preceding events of the poem and the foreshadowing they provide. What events will occur after the poem's end? How is it appropriate or inappropriate to the nature of this poem for the narrative to end with much yet to be accomplished (e.g. Teiresias' suggested voyage)?

Sample Analytical Paper Topics

Topic #1

Hospitality is a central motif of the *Odyssey* that focuses on the behavior of both hosts and their guests. Discuss examples of host-guest relations as they exist throughout the poem.

Outline

I. Thesis Statement: *Homer suggests both positive and negative commentary on his own world through the examples of hospitality that pervade the* Odyssey.

II. Scenes of Positive Hospitality

    A. Telemachus' treatment of Athene (Book I)

    B. Nestor's reception of Telemachus (Book III)

    C. Menelaus' reception of Telemachus (Book IV)

    D. Odysseus among the Phaeaceans (Books VI-VIII, XIII)

    E. Eumaeus' reception of Odysseus (Book XIV)

III. Scenes of Negative Hospitality

    A. The suitors in Odysseus' house (I, II, XVIII-XXII)

    B. Polyphemus' cave (Book IX)

    C. Circe's abode (Book X)

IV. Common elements of both types of hospitality scenes

V. Subtle and overt contrasts between both types of hospitality scenes

VI. Homer's implied messages about his society in both types of hospitality scenes

Topic #2

Deception and the revelation of identity are two motifs that accompany each other throughout the *Odyssey*. Analyze the various scenes from the poem that center around these motifs and explore the significance of the motifs' variations that occur from scene to scene.

Outline

I.   Thesis Statement: *Homer provides a subtle commentary on his characters through the changes and variations that accompany each scene depicting disguise and the subsequent revelation of a character's identity.*

II. Athene's Disguises As:
  A. Mentes (Book I)
  B. Mentor and Telemachus (Book II)
  C. Mentor (Book III)
  D. The young Phaeacean girl (Book VII)
  E. The young shepard (Book XIII)
  F. Mentor (Book XXII)

III. Odysseus' Disguises As:
  A. A beggar in Troy (Book IV)
  B. The unknown wanderer
  C. Nobody (Book IX)
  D. The innocent victim (in Circe's cottage; Book X)
  E. The lost wanderer (to Athene; Book XIII)
  F. Old beggar from Crete (Books XIV, XVI, XIX, XXII, XXIII)

IV. Analysis of modes of deception

V.   Significance of revelation scenes

VI. Similarities and differences among revelation scenes

Topic #3

Characters often relate large blocks of narrative to fellow characters. Examine the stories told by characters during the course of the *Odyssey*. What do the characters reveal about themselves during the course of their narratives? What are the hidden purposes of the characters who act as storytellers? What do they hope to achieve through the narration of their stories?

Outline

I.   Thesis Statement: *Storytellers throughout the* Odyssey *introduce aspects of themselves during their narratives not revealed elsewhere, such as personality traits, hidden agendas, etc.*

II. Long narratives delivered by characters
   A. Nestor (Book III)
   B. Menelaus (Book IV)
   C. Proteus (Book IV)
   D. Helen (Book IV)
   E. Demodocus (Book VIII)
   F. Odysseus (Books IX-XII, XIV, XIX, and XXIV)
   G. Souls of the Deceased (Book XI)
   H. Eumaeus (Book XV)
   I. Agamemnon (Book XXIV)
   J. Amphimedon (Book XXIV)

III. Hidden purposes of the storytellers

IV. Personality traits revealed during their stories

V.   Decisions made by the storytellers based upon their audiences

Topic #4

An important subplot of the *Odyssey* is the assassination of Agamemnon. Explore the relationships, overt and subtle, between this subplot and the main plot of Odysseus' homecoming.

Outline

I.   *Thesis Statement: There is a significant thematic relationship between Agamemnon's family and Odysseus' family. Each family member experiences a fate that is diametrically opposed to that of his parallel counterpart.*

II. Chief references to Agamemnon's murder
   A. Zeus (Book I)
   B. Athene (Book I)
   C. Nestor (Book III)
   D. Menelaus (Book IV)
   E. Agamemnon (Books XI, XXIV)

III. Parallels between Agamemnon's family and Odysseus' family

IV. Significance of the differences between their family situations

V.   Purpose of the subplot's shadowing of the main plot

SECTION FOUR

Bibliography

Quotations of the *Odyssey* are taken from the following translation:

Homer. *The Odyssey of Homer.* Tr. Richmond Lattimore. New York: Harper & Row, 1975.

In addition, Lattimore's introduction was indispensable to this study. The following works were also consulted often during the course of this work:

Aurbach, Erich. *Mimesis: The Representation of Reality in Western Literature.* Tr. Willard R. Trask. Princeton: Princeton University Press, 1953.

Camps, W. A. *An Introduction to Homer.* Oxford: Clarendon Press, 1980.

Lord, Albert B. *The Singer of Tales.* Cambridge: Harvard University Press, 1964.

Scott, John A. *The Unity of Homer.* Sather Classical Lectures. Berkeley: The University of California Press, 1921.

Tillyard, E. M. W. *The English Epic and its Background.* New York: Barnes & Noble, Inc., 1954.